The Secret of
Natural Readers

The Secret of Natural Readers

How Preschool Children
Learn to Read

Ada Anbar

PRAEGER

Westport, Connecticut
London

Library of Congress Cataloging-in-Publication Data

Anbar, Ada, 1935–
    The secret of natural readers : how preschool children learn to read /
Ada Anbar.
        p. cm.
    Includes bibliographical references and index.
    ISBN 0–275–98424–9 (alk. paper)
    1. Reading (Preschool) 2. Literacy.   I. Title.
LB1140.5.R4A515   2004
372.4—dc22   2004050586

British Library Cataloguing in Publication Data is available.

Library of Congress Catalog Card Number: 2004050586
ISBN: 0–275–98424–9

First published in 2004

Praeger Publishers, 88 Post Road West, Westport, CT 06881
An imprint of Greenwood Publishing Group, Inc.
www.praeger.com

Printed in the United States of America

The paper used in this book complies with the
Permanent Paper Standard issued by the National
Information Standards Organization (Z39.48–1984).

10   9   8   7   6   5   4   3   2   1

To Michael
for a beautiful life

Until 6,000 years ago,
Everybody was illiterate,
Then reading was invented.
—The author

To write and read comes
by nature.
—William Shakespeare,
Much Ado About Nothing

Preschool children learn best through play.
Natural reading development does not replace play,
It is based on play!
—The author

Contents

Preface

I first stumbled on preschool reading capability many years ago when a friend asked me to teach her five-year-old son to read. We were living in Israel at the time, and my friend's family was planning a yearlong visit to the United States. Concerned that her son would be poorly prepared for first grade, she asked me to give him a leg up and teach him beginning reading. And so the boy came over to our home three times a week during that summer month to take his Hebrew reading lessons.

My own son, who was three years old at the time, asked to sit with us and listen to the sessions. I agreed. And then my friend's two-year-old daughter, who thought this sounded like fun, asked to join us too. I gave in to her request on the condition that she behaved well. She did. And so the three children and myself spent some pleasant hours during that summer month on our balcony, surrounded by pink, white, and red geraniums, helping the child learn to read. By the end of the summer, the five-year-old boy went to the United States, and I continued to help my son occasionally with his reading. To my surprise, by age four, Ran was able to read from all of his Hebrew picture books.

I was a teacher of emotionally disturbed children at the time, working at a rehabilitation hospital with children who had to be removed from their homes because of behavior problems.

A few years later, we moved to the United States, and when our younger son started nursery school—one of the best university nursery schools in the country—I fell in love with that place. I became fascinated with early childhood education, with the breadth and depth of development that occurs in the early years of life. And I decided to change my specialty to working with preschool children. Helping prevent problems from developing would be more rewarding, I thought, than trying to ameliorate problems in later years.

Meanwhile, my younger son was learning to read English and Hebrew (we spoke Hebrew at home and English outside the home). Intuitively supporting his literacy development, I was curious to see if he would become an early reader like his older brother. As it turned out, by age four Ariel was a fluent reader of English picture books. I admit that I had been neglecting his Hebrew reading development by then.

During the 1980s, America was changing its attitude toward early reading development. There was a growing acceptance of early readers and a burgeoning fascination with the topic. Working then toward my doctoral degree in early childhood education, I was challenged one day "to do something with those children"—a group of preschool readers my adviser had identified and videotaped. Reportedly, these children had learned to read by themselves and were regarded by my adviser and their parents to be unusually precocious. Having raised two early readers myself, bright kids, albeit not uncommonly gifted, I was interested in the topic and felt intellectually challenged. Curious to find out how these children had acquired their early reading ability, and what kind of developmental process they experienced, I made this question the focus of my doctoral study.

So how do three- and four-year-old children become capable readers without formal instruction? How *can* they do it? While many schoolchildren have difficulty with literacy, these preschoolers seemed to find it easy. Moreover, researchers found that hundreds of thousands of American youngsters enter first grade knowing how to read (for political reasons this finding has not received much publicity). While some children are formally taught, many are not. So what is the secret of their accomplishment; do they really have a unique innate talent for reading, as some parents believe? *The Secret of Natural Readers* provides the answer to this important question.

Recounting the story of six preschool children, all capable readers before age four with no systematic instruction, this book illustrates how they acquired their early ability. Rich with anecdotes depicting daily life scenes, a chronicled step-by-step account of their learning process is presented. This account offers a new paradigm for early reading development, showing there is much more to it than formal instruction or an unusual talent. In today's literate environment, early reading ability can be achieved naturally, playfully, during routine daily activities, with little pressure and much fun.

My early conclusion has been recently confirmed on a national level. Following three decades of research on early reading development, and new insight from brain research, the National Association for the Education of Young Children (NAEYC) and the International Reading Association (IRA) are now recognizing the critical importance of the early years for the development of literacy, and, moreover, the effect of this early development on the standards of children's achievements. These two national organizations are now calling on all parents and preschool teachers to encourage children's literacy development from an early age. And numerous programs are now being developed to offer guidance on how to do that.

The Secret of Natural Readers joins this effort. This book provides a documented model for action: an evidence-based approach that is grounded on the actual reading development of accomplished young readers who were never formally taught. This approach is based on play, and it is developmentally appropriate. It can be applied at home and/or in a preschool setting.

Acknowledgments

I would like to express my deep gratitude to the following people:

The late Professor Edith Dowley, founder and director of Bing Nursery School at Stanford University, for introducing me to the field of early childhood education, and teaching me about the importance of play in young children's lives.

The late William Eller, professor of reading instruction at the University at Buffalo, and former president of the International Reading Association, who encouraged me to take on the fight for preschool reading while preparing me for the uphill struggle to change the public's attitude.

Special thanks are due to the parents and children who are profiled in this book (their names have been changed to protect their privacy). They are the true heroes of this work and made it all possible. Patiently sharing with me their experiences, I will always be indebted to them. The gracious invitations to their homes and cups of coffee that we shared will be fondly remembered.

Thanks to Mary Read and Dorothy Golden for making valuable suggestions.

Many thanks to my editors: Susan Slesinger, a wonderful, capable person, who swiftly moved the work through the initial hurdles, and Denise Quimby, who guided the project through its bound-book stage.

And last but not least, I would like to thank my family: my children, Ran, Hannah, Ariel, and Marni, for giving me insight into natural reading development at home; my grandchildren, Josh, Rebecca, Ellie, Yoni, Nathaniel, and Naomi, for further enhancing my insight; and, most importantly, my husband, Michael, for standing by me through the long gestation period of this book, patiently reading and editing the many drafts of the manuscript, and being my computer expert.

Part I

By Way of Introduction

Chapter One

———————

Reading Has a History

> The acquisition of language is doubtless the greatest intellectual feat anyone of us is ever to perform.
> —Leonard Bloomfield, Introduction
> to the *Study of Language*

Reading and writing are among the basic skills that children must acquire in their early years. Reading is a key to learning, a means to open doors to knowledge. Writing is the tool we use to record information, augment memory, and communicate our feelings and thoughts. These two skills—the written side of language—are so basic to contemporary life that any serious deficiency in either of them is a real handicap. Illiteracy involves the risk of being mentally underdeveloped and culturally disconnected; it also severely reduces the chance for a productive adulthood in contemporary society.

It was not always like this. The social value of reading and writing has changed over time. Throughout most of human existence, literacy was of little importance for the majority of people. It is a relatively recent concept that has gone through many transformations. And the story behind its proliferation from obscure embryonic beginnings to its current universal practice provides a fascinating account, involving culture, religion, technology, commerce, politics, human ingenuity, and, more than anything else, human drive for growth and development.

In this chapter, I draw a brief outline of this evolutionary story. It will give the reader a perspective on literacy, an appreciation for the progress that has been achieved so far, and better insight into contemporary issues concerning literacy and its development. Understanding the transformations that literacy underwent in the past will enhance our ability to work through changes that may take place in the future. Parents, who have a strong impact on their children's education and development, especially in the early years, early childhood educators, and others who are interested in young children's development are likely to benefit from this panoramic view. It will increase their ability to make wise decisions regarding children's reading and writing development. So let us begin our tour and start from the beginning.

IN THE BEGINNING

When was the written language invented? Why and where was it invented? And, how has this invention affected human life? During the approximately 3 million years of human evolution, until just a few thousand years ago, mankind did not know to read or write. Mostly occupied with the struggle for survival, the development of oral language, and beginning culture, prehistoric man—our hunter-gatherer ancestor—was absolutely illiterate. There was apparently neither the need nor the desire to develop and use a written language. The earliest evidence we have of recorded information on a physical surface are bones with tally marks scratched on them, dated from around thirty thousand years ago.

Paintings are another form of early records. Magnificent paintings of large animals chased by hunting men, drawn more than twenty thousand years ago, can be found in different parts of the world. Some of the most exquisite examples are located in the cave of Lascaux in southwestern France, the cave of Altamira in northern Spain, and in the recently discovered Chauvet cave in southeastern France. A common explanation postulates that these paintings were used, through a form of sympathetic magic, to ensure success in the hunt.

But the move from a hunting-based to an agriculture-based economy brought about major changes in the lifestyle of the people. When civilization emerged, and small settlements grew into villages and towns, the mystical cave paintings were no longer useful in the daily organization of life in the new society. The growing complexity of town and city life, settled by strangers who often did not know one another, required a new system for the organization of social structure. It is commonly assumed that this new requirement was the impetus for the development of writing. There was no sudden leap, however, from cave paintings to script writing. For thousands of years in prehistoric time, entrepreneurs in the Middle East were recording their business deals with clay tokens modeled in sixteen distinctive shapes (at first "plain" then more "complex") such as cones, spheres, disks, cylinders, or tetrahedrons, each representing a precise quantity of a product. These symbols developed in time into a pictographic script.[1]

Writing was probably developed to keep records of ownership, stored food, and astronomical events (to optimize sowing time), and to aid in tax collection. Writing also enhanced commercial transactions. But most importantly, writing was essential for the establishment and maintenance of law and order. This was particularly important in the new urban communities, among people who moved away from tribal life with its tight social structure. Once a law was put in writing and publicly displayed (on a large slab of stone or the wall of a monument, as was customary), it provided the necessary regulation for the new society. It also protected the weak from oppression by the strong, to repeat Hammurabi's words, "The written laws protect everybody."[2]

It appears that early writing was also associated with the concept of a deity. In many cultures, writing was at first revered as a gift from the gods. And priests were among the first to use script, perhaps as a means to control the population through the written words of the god. (Think of Moses coming down from the mountain holding the Ten Commandments carved in stone.) The priests used script also to praise their gods and kings and pray for their benevolence and protection. Prophylactic amulets with inscriptions were very common all over the ancient world.

Where was this innovation first developed, and how did it spread to the rest of the world? The earliest piece of writing found so far, dated at about 3500 BC, has been uncovered in Uruk, an ancient Sumerian city in Mesopotamia (now Iraq) on a tablet of solid limestone. It is believed to be a tax account. Although different writing systems evolved independently in other regions of the world—India, the islands of the Aegean Sea, China, and pre-Columbian America, to name a few—the ancient Sumerians are credited with being the first-known literate people. The invention of writing was their gift to humanity. This invention not only helped in the organization of a new and more complex society, it revolutionized all human activity. Because writing begets reading, these activities engender each other. And the highly developed Mesopotemian cultures had much to write about. And so a new phase of human progression could begin.

THE BRIDGE TO HISTORY

"Script was the last achievement of prehistoric man; with it, he crosses the bridge to history," wrote Felix Reichmann of Cornell University.[3] Once writing was invented, humanity began to progress at a rapid pace, unparalleled in prehistoric times. Without writing, the sum total knowledge of each isolated region was limited by the memories of its oldest people and by what each generation could discover anew for itself. With writing, it was possible to begin to accumulate knowledge, and one generation after another could learn from the experience of the past.

Yet, as is often the case with new innovations, writing was not unanimously embraced at first. A famous Egyptian legend, for instance, tells that when the god Thoth revealed his discovery of writing to King Thamos, the king denounced it as an enemy of civilization: "Children and young people," protested the monarch, "who had hitherto been forced to apply themselves diligently to learn and retain whatever was taught them, would cease to apply themselves, and would neglect to exercise their memories."[4] Plato voiced a similar concern. And there was some truth to that apprehension. Fortunately, the advantages of writing surpassed its apparent disadvantages, and the pressure to progress prevailed.

While it is accepted that script had a polygenetic origin, its development in most regions followed a similar pattern. First there was "picture writing," or pictograms. Then came "idea pictures," or ideograms. Next came syllabic writing, based on the sound of words rather than their image. And that writing system evolved into an alphabetic script. The progression was always toward increased simplification with fewer and fewer signs to be remembered (with the exception of the Chinese and Japanese scripts, which belong to different writing systems from those in Western cultures. Chinese writing has a logographic script in which each word has its own graph, requiring a literate Chinese to know several thousand graphs. Japanese writing is a mixed system, partly logographic and partly phonographic.)[5]

FROM HIEROGLYPHS TO ABC

As the invention of writing was spreading throughout the ancient world, two regions stood out in the extent of their literacy production, namely, Mesopotamia and Egypt. The Mesopotamian people (which included the Sumerians, Akkadians, Babylonians, and Assyrians) developed the cuneiform script, composed of slim wedge-shaped elements, using wedge-ended pieces of reed to imprint the symbols on wet clay tablets. Only a few hundred miles away, the ancient Egyptians developed the hieroglyphic script, an ornamental picture writing, inscribed on walls of tombs and temples, that was used extensively to provide permanent records and decoration. Writing was used also to keep administrative records, commercial contracts and deeds, and official and private correspondence. By 3000 BC, both the cuneiform and the hieroglyphic scripts were in full use.

Over time, Egypt and Mesopotamia created impressive bodies of literature. Much of the Egyptian writing that has survived over the millennia was found on the walls of temples and tombs and funerary equipment. What has been preserved is largely associated, therefore, with the topic of death and the afterlife. Many copies of the Book of the Dead, for example, were found, designed to assist the deceased in the painful travel through the netherworld. The Mesopotamian clay tablets have been much better preserved. And about half a million tablets have been found dealing with all aspects of life, including schoolbooks, dictionaries, scientific and religious texts, and long epic poems about the creation of the world, the fall of man, and the Great Flood. Other tablets dealt with medicine, astrology, mathematical calculations, and the law.

The cuneiform script was very successful and was adopted by many peoples in the Middle East. The hieroglyphic script served well mainly the Egyptian culture. And both scripts went through several transformations over the millennia, adapting to the evolving needs of their cultures. Libraries full of clay tablets were found in Mesopotamia. But in general, literacy in ancient times belonged to the priests, the professional scribes, and a layer of the aristocracy. The majority of people did not learn to read or write, except for probable memorization of publicly displayed laws. (Though there was nothing to prevent a bright boy, whose parents were interested and able to afford it, from receiving elementary instruction in reading and writing from a tutor.)

Scribes, who received their extensive training in special schools located adjacent to temples, staffed the civil administration, the royal court, and the temples. The general public hired these scribes' services as needed. The majority of the population, who had no formal schooling, received their education within the family, and through the oral transmission of the culture—its laws, festivals, and religious ceremonies. Often they would listen to the readings and storytelling of those who could read. Both civilizations used their extensive literature as reading material for the education of the upper class.

While a version of the cuneiform was still used in Mesopotamia during the first century AD, the cuneiform and hieroglyphic scripts gradually reached their limits. And after three thousand years of use, the time was ripe for a new stage in the evolution of writing and reading.

The Invention of the Alphabet

Between the eighteenth and the sixteenth centuries BC, there was much unrest in the Middle East, including massive uprooting of established cultural and ethnic patterns. Wars, population pressures, and famines drove many western Semites along the eastern shores of the Mediterranean from one land to another. Commerce became a major factor in the economy. And there was a growing need to develop a new script that would be simpler and quicker to use, easy to learn, and more accessible to wider segments of the population. There was a need for a script that could enable the transcription of words from one language to another even when not knowing the meaning of the words. It is suggested that this climate gave birth to the alphabetic script.

The new innovation must have started with the realization that all syllables are made up of a relatively small number of elementary sounds. Most languages have no more than twenty to thirty of these basic sounds. Once this fact was recognized, the alphabetic principle was discovered. The alphabet is the simplest form of script to be invented. Instead of memorizing the symbolic presentations of thousands of words, alphabetic script uses fewer than thirty signs to represent the most basic sounds of any language; one symbol for each sound. Learning the alphabet is literally child's play compared with the years required for mastering the cuneiform or hieroglyphic scripts. This new system was so easy to learn and adopt that before long it was transmitted to most cultures, though there was a long overlapping period in which hieroglyphs, cuneiform, and beginning alphabetic script were used in parallel, probably for different types of text. The alphabetic script continues to be the most widely used writing system in the world today.

Where was this new script first developed? And who were the people who helped develop it? Andrew Robinson of Eton College refers to this question as the "riddle of the alphabet,"[6] saying that many questions about its origins have yet to be answered. But it is clear that of the many western Semites who contributed to this innovation (including also the Mesopotamians and the Egyptians), the final credit goes to the Phoenicians. They gave the system its basic form, perfecting the alphabet of twenty-two consonants, and they standardized the script to be read from right to left. The Phoenician alphabet was in full use in Byblos, a Canaanite town north of modern Beirut, around 1300 BC. As the hub of commercial activity between the East and the West, this town provided a fertile ground for the development and exchange of new ideas.

The rapid acceptance of the alphabet played a major role in the spread of literacy. More people could spare the relatively short time required to learn the simple new script, and more people acquired reading ability. Consequently, more texts were written, and the ranks of literate people began to swell.

LITERACY GOES TO THE MASSES

Yet it was the Greeks and the Judeans who made the greatest contribution to the advancement of literacy. As the Phoenician merchants were having commercial contact with their Greek colleagues along the shores of the Mediterranean, the new alphabet reached Greece around 1000 BC, and the Greeks added characters for vowels, making the script more compatible with the sounds of the Greek language. The Greek version of the Phoenician alphabet remained the basis for Western alphabetic systems developed since then.

But there was another way by which Ancient Greece influenced the spread of literacy. The Greeks created an impressive body of secular literature, including dramas, histories, and philosophy books, which attracted wide interest. Describing universal themes, Greek literature showed a profound understanding of human nature that still inspires today. Some of the greatest Western philosophers lived in ancient Greece in the fifth century BC, including Socrates, Plato, and Aristotle. The Greek philosophers were among the first to propose the idea of communal schools and compulsory education for all children. Their writings had a great impact on Western civilization from ancient times to the present, spreading the interest in reading.

Furthermore, Athens, "the eye of Greece," conceived the idea of democracy; the notion that every freeborn adult male citizen should have a say in the running of the state. So, since the fifth century BC, freeborn citizens were expected to be educated and receive at least elementary instruction, including basic proficiency in reading. But schools were not yet publicly supported, and thus were privately organized and run, with Athenian education remaining the responsibility of the family's patriarch. Fathers paid the bill and determined the length of their offspring's education. Often this was carried out at home with the help of a *pedagogue*, the common child's tutor.

Meanwhile, as the Phoenicians were busy spreading the new alphabet, the Israelites, their neighbors to the south, were creating the Bible—a compilation of sacred writings that would in time become the spiritual anchor of that people, and later Europe's most universal text for reading. Following a national disaster in 538 BC, people of the southern Israelite kingdom, the Judeans, were obsessed by a national fervor to preserve and perpetuate their culture. To secure that goal, they started a campaign of mass education, establishing houses of learning throughout the land, where scribes taught the people (only males) free of charge to read and study the Torah. Young and old started to come to these centers, and by 75 BC even schools for "babies" were organized, teaching young children to read the Pentateuch. Shortly thereafter, elementary schools became obligatory for all six-year-old Judean boys, teaching writing, reading, arithmetic, and the law. This Jewish tradition of love of learning from an early age, which started in the second century BC, has been continuously perpetuated till modern times. So we see how once the alphabetic system linked up with the concept of democracy, as it did in Greece and Judea, the ability to read and write began to spill over from the exclusive domain of the scribal, priestly, and aristocratic class to the rest of the population.

LITERACY AND THE CHURCH

What was the story of literacy since the days of ancient Greece and Judea? When Rome began to dominate the world, it adopted the Etruscan alphabet, an Italian offshoot of the Greek script, and with the expansion of the empire, the alphabet spread all over Europe. Rome also embraced much of Greek culture, including its literature and educational system, thus raising the public's incentive to become literate.

However, the rise of Christianity modified the course of European education. The church was antagonistic to the dissemination of "pagan" thought. And once it took control of the European educational system, it banned the study of Greek literature. The Christian Bible became increasingly the main text for European reading and the sole source of moral life—"the mirror in which men must learn to see themselves." By the ninth century AD, the first primers appeared, containing religious selections to be taught to children, including the Creed, the Lord's

Prayer, the Ten Commandments, and a few Psalms. ABC books for teaching reading were also published.

But relatively few European children became literate. The Christian education of children, who were not of aristocratic families or future clergy, was irregular. Once the child was baptized, no particular education was required, and any learning that occurred was in the hands of the family. There was an overall decline of interest and appreciation of literacy. Reading, writing, and humanistic studies moved to the cloisters and monasteries. Even the nobility was excluded from the world of literacy, thus some of Europe's medieval kings did not find it necessary to learn to read and write, choosing to remain illiterate.

THE RENAISSANCE

And then, beginning in the fourteenth century and extending to the seventeenth century, there was a great revival of art, literature, and learning. Like a fresh breeze of air, the spirit of the Renaissance began to sweep over Europe, restoring interest in humanistic education and reviving Greek and Latin studies. In the fifteenth century, commerce began to expand, and the monasteries and cloisters no longer monopolized learning. Learned individuals were now expected to get involved with the affairs of the city and the good of the community. Indenture of servants, deeding of property, evidence at trials, and correspondence with peers, all required widespread reading and writing ability. Shortly, monastic schools started to close and urban schools grew popular. While public clerks continued to function for some time as petitioners or advocates, providing the general public with needed service, the personal ability to read and write became increasingly desirable. Literacy became the passport to success and stature. And it gradually became a necessary skill for managing daily affairs.

THE PRINTING PRESS

Yet of all the developments during the Renaissance, the one that did the most to dramatically advance the spread of literacy was the reinvention of the printing press. (Printing with movable types had been invented earlier in China and Korea but that invention did not spread to the West and thus remained confined to Buddhist regions.) Prior to the fifteenth century, books had been written and copied by hand, or were printed by a laborious process of carving each page as a separate woodcut. Once movable metal type was introduced and the printing press was developed, bookmaking became, by far, a simpler, faster, and less-expensive process.

Developed in Strasbourg by Johann Gutenberg, with the financial backing of a lawyer acquaintance named Johann Fust, and introduced in 1446, the invention of the printing press revolutionized literacy. It engendered an immediate and rapid diffusion of printed material at affordable cost. And this was followed by a greater incentive to become literate, and consequently to write new texts for the growing readership.

The printing press enabled two other major social transformations that had a tremendous impact on the spread and evolution of literacy: the Protestant Reformation and the rise of modern science. Once the Bible was readily available to the general public in its native language and at reasonable cost, Martin Luther declared, in 1519, that every man has the right to read the Bible for oneself and discover its meaning. This idea became one of the fundamental tenets of Protestantism. And for many believers it became the compelling reason for learning to read. As Martin Luther recommended, "Let the Scriptures be the chief and most frequently used reading book, both primary and high schools and the very young should be kept in the gospels. Is it not proper and right that every human being, by the time he has reached his tenth year, should be familiar with the holy gospels, in which the very core and marrow of his life is bound?"[7]

Furthermore, with the help of the new printing press, Luther could now disseminate his ideas to the masses and reach an international audience. His ninety-five theses, or propositions for change—first nailed to the door of a church—which initiated the Protestant Reformation, were quickly translated from the Latin into German and other European languages, and printed and circulated widely throughout Europe.

The translation of the Bible to German and other European languages was followed by the extensive translation of other important books from the scholarly Greek and Latin into the vernacular. The ability to study the written classical texts, as well as books written by other scholars, contributed also to the rise of modern science. More people could now develop independent and critical thinking capability.

And so, by the nineteenth century, more than half the population in western Europe and America had some competence in reading and writing. Toward the end of the century, compulsory schooling was slowly introduced. And in 1918, school attendance became the civic duty of American youth, with public schooling provided all over the country. Some level of literacy becoming more or less universal.

CONCLUSION

Several conclusions can be drawn from this bird's eye view on the evolution of literacy:

- First, historically, it appears that literacy has never been a fixed, firm concept with a rigid definition. On the contrary, literacy appears to be a dynamic concept with changing societal expectations. It is a concept that emerges out of life's conditions and is continuously being shaped by them. As the needs of society change, the standards of literacy change, the definition of literacy often changes, the script may change, instructional methodologies may change, and a person who is considered literate in one era may be considered illiterate in another.
- Second, literacy appears to be in a continuous march forward, vertically and horizontally. The standard of achievement is continuously raised and the circle of literate people is continuously expanding.
- Third, technology appears to have a continuous impact on the evolution of literacy. From its inception, a succession of technological innovations helped shape the form of script and facilitate the spread of literacy to an ever-widening segment of the population.
- Fourth, the changing standards of literacy and societal expectations reflect the political structure of society, its economy, and its level of development: the more devel-

oped and democratic the society, the greater the need for literacy; the wider the literate segment of its population, the higher its literacy standards.

Clearly, literacy has made immense strides in a relatively short period of time. From a world of absolute illiteracy less than six thousand years ago, we have reached a stage of development where reading and writing ability have become essential for survival. Today, literacy is the key to personal knowledge, economic independence, culture, and intellectual freedom. It is no longer the domain of the upper class but a publicly supported and necessary skill for all productive adults in a developed society. Immense strides were made in the past and there is little doubt that enormous developments await us in the future. As Nila Banton Smith, the noted reading scholar, wrote, "While our accomplishments have been very great, indeed, it may be that we have only penetrated the first layer, the troposphere, so to speak. Undoubtedly, brilliant new insights will be revealed, ingenious new techniques of experimentation will be evolved, more effective methods and materials will be devised. Possibilities of such development portend opportunities for unlimited achievement in the future."[8] In the next chapter, we will focus our attention on the United States and in particular on reading development of young children.

Chapter Two

When Do Children Learn to Read?

Setting a child aside until elementary school age and then saying that now education begins is like taking a withered or withering sprout and suddenly giving it large amounts of fertilizer, putting it in the sunlight and flooding it with water. It is too late for the withered sprout.

—Shinichi Suzuki, *From Plato to Piaget*

BEFORE THE ERA OF COMPULSORY EDUCATION

Education in America was at first influenced by European practice, in particular by education in England. But, because of the frontier conditions, many instructional adaptations needed to be made. And so, up until the mid-nineteenth century when compulsory education began to spread all over the United States, children's education was the responsibility of parents. In part, this resulted out of necessity because the school and the church were often not readily accessible, and, more importantly, because of a raging controversy over the state's right to assume educational authority and consequently to levy additional taxes.

At what age did American children start learning to read and write? Before the days of compulsory schooling, the answer was relatively simple. Since parents had the responsibility for their children's education, they made the decision at what age to start teaching them. And they probably began the process whenever they felt the children were ready to learn, and they (the parents) were ready to teach them—either directly or with the help of others.

Many anecdotal reports from the last three centuries, often found in diaries, describe three-, four-, and five-year-old children, sometimes even younger, acquiring reading ability. "When I was two years old I began to be taken to the Quaker meeting as well as to school. . . .When I was three years old I could read very well," recorded Elizabeth Buffum Chace in the nineteenth-century diary she and her sister, Lucy, kept.[1] Edward and Elaine Gordon, the authors of *Literacy in America*, recount the story of a nineteenth-century child named Lucy Larcom who grew up in Charlestown, Massachusetts, near Boston, "She started attending 'school' at age two, 'as other children about us did,' kept by a neighbor everyone called 'Aunt Hannah.' . . . [C]onducted in her kitchen or sitting room . . . Lucy learned her 'letters' standing at Aunt Hannah's knee while she pointed them out in the spelling book with a pin."[2] The Gordons also recount, "In seventeenth- and eighteenth-century America a preschool child probably would have first been introduced to *The New England Primer* at home. The alphabet instructional method was the sole teaching method used."[3]

Young children were taught to read by schoolmasters, their parents, older siblings, or relatives. Families who could afford it often hired a tutor or governess. Dame schools, run by women who were teaching small groups of children manners and basic reading in their homes, were also popular. Some urban districts established small private community schools. Others sponsored quasi-public grammar schools, and many churches ran small schools for their parishioners. Schooling was immensely diverse. But in general, the early years were considered the appropriate time and the home the right place for beginning reading and writing development. As Edmund Burke Huey, the first American psychologist of reading instruction, explained in 1908, "The home is the natural place for learning to read, in connection with the child's introduction to literature through story telling, picture reading, etc. The child will make much use of reading and writing in his plays, using both pictures and words."[4]

And while in colonial America youngsters learned to read by first mastering the letters and syllables phonetically and then hearing scripture passages read to them again and again with the reader pointing at each word, methods of instruction continuously evolved. The environment has become increasingly more literate, and by the beginning of the twentieth century, it was recognized that early reading development was often quite informal, including much incidental learning in conjunction with other activities in which the children engaged. As Huey explained, "The child makes endless questioning about the names of things, as every mother knows. He is concerned also about the printed notices, signs, titles, visiting cards, etc., that come in his way, and should be told what these 'say' when he makes inquiry. It is surprising how large a stock of printed or written words a child will gradually come to recognize in this way."[5]

It must be noted, however, that up until the twentieth century there was a high degree of illiteracy. Many people could function productively, under the economic conditions of those days, without having reading and writing skills. And there was a strong resistance from the public to the introduction of secular ("godless") state-supported education for all, which was perceived to be an intrusion into parental privilege, and a cause for increased taxes. So, many children, in particular from poor families, were not given the opportunity to learn to read or write. As the Gordons write, "During the first 60 years of the nineteenth century, children raised in the northeastern states who received any literacy education did so mainly through private instruction at home or through sectarian institutions. . . . Societal conditions withheld literacy from the majority of children, though by the Civil War (1860) a gradual cultural shift had occurred favoring broader literacy opportunities for both boys and girls."[6]

THE BEGINNING OF COMPULSORY EDUCATION

When public schooling became mandatory nationwide in 1918, attitudes toward children's reading development began to change. Schoolteachers rather than parents were now responsible for teaching children to read. And since a child's schooling started at age six, reading instruction became associated with that age. There is nothing magical about age six, and children have been learning a great deal before they reach that age. But teaching large groups of children is easier when they are six years old. They require less individual attention. They can separate comfortably from their parents. And they can sit still for longer periods of time.

READING READINESS

And so a new rationale began to emerge about the optimal age to start teaching reading. This rationale was soon backed up by a new theoretical concept: reading readiness. The notion was that children should first reach an appropriate mental age before they start learning to read. Before they reach that age, many will fail to learn, said the proponents of this new concept.

What was the justification for this new concept? Children had been learning to read before age six for a long time, so why come up with this new rationalization? For one, public mandatory education resulted in large classrooms. Children were now taught to read in large groups, sometimes with as many as forty children per group. Since children's pace of learning varies, with some learning faster than others, behavior problems began to surface. Teachers started having difficulty in teaching some of the children. And the concept of reading readiness became very useful for explaining the variations in youngsters' learning abilities—irrespective of socioeconomic background, individual aptitude, and early experiences.

Moreover, at the beginning of the twentieth century, the concept of maturation had just been popularized by the writings of Arnold Gesell, the noted physician and authority on child development. Gesell addressed at length the topic of maturation, describing the distinct developmental stages in the maturation process that all children must go through. His theory provided the simplest—and most quoted—explanation for first graders who experienced difficulties in learning to read. These children were simply not yet ready to learn when their instruction began, said the proponents of that theory. They had not yet reached the appropriate level of mental maturation (or "neural ripening" as Gesell sometimes described it) required for reading. No one had considered at the time the possibility of poor instruction, the negative effect of excessively large classes, or the inappropriateness of existing teaching materials, as pointed out by Dolores Durkin, the noted early reading researcher.[7]

Furthermore, the new testing movement that became popular in the 1920s and 1930s and the growing use of quantitative measurement of children's achievements contributed to the change in attitude toward beginning reading instruction. "One in every six children failed at the end of the first semester in first grade, and one in every eight failed at the end of the second semester," declared Mary Reed in 1927;[8] this contributed to a climate of panic in the educational establishment and the public.

Then a landmark article by Mabel Morphet and Carleton Washburne, published in 1931, crystallized this new thinking, concluding that by postponing reading instruction until children reach the mental age of six and a half, chances of failure would be greatly decreased.[9] Following the publication of this article, the concept of reading readiness was put into wide practice. "Educators everywhere began to awaken to the needs for attention to readiness at the beginning level. . . . The fire once kindled soon became a conflagration," wrote Nila Banton Smith, a reading education leader of the twentieth century. [10] Although objections were raised to this conclusion, the authority of Washburne, who was superintendent of the Winnetka, Illinois, school system and a prominent leader of the progressive education movement, overruled them.

Soon a whole industry developed around the concept of reading readiness. Reading readiness tests were prepared to determine which children were ready to start learning to read. Reading readiness programs were introduced, and then reading readiness workbooks were added. By the period 1938 to 1940, the concept of reading readiness reached its zenith, with the enthusiastic support of the publishing industry, the educational establishment, and parents.

Anecdotal reports about youngsters who learn to read at age three and four kept circulating. But there was an overt attempt to discourage such early development and dismiss reported cases as rare and of little relevance to the general population. In fact, during the first half of the twentieth century, when psychology became influential and the nation became sensitive to children's emotional and social development, comments about early readers often had a negative connotation. Precocity was associated with poor physical health and emotional disorder. "Early ripe, early rot" was a common slogan at the time. And teachers of young children were advised about reading: "Don't do anything with it!"

Within a few decades, parents felt too intimidated to encourage their youngsters' reading development at home. Persuaded that preschoolers are not yet mentally ready for reading, they shied away from reading-related interactions with them—except for storybook readings—fearing they might cause harm by a too early stimulation. Needless to say, many parents probably found it convenient to relegate their children's reading development to the professional schoolteacher. By 1955, psychologist Sidney Pressey felt it was necessary to criticize this attitude, remarking that "[t]here is a general belief, fostered in this country by most psychologists and 'progressive' educators, that intellectual precocity is somehow not quite healthy, is almost always a hazard to good social adjustment, and should be slowed down rather than facilitated."[11]

THE PENDULUM SWINGS BACK

But then came *Sputnik*, and a dramatic change in attitude swept over the country, compelling educators and parents to approach early literacy with less apprehension. A number of reasons brought about this attitudinal change. The shocking news of the launching of *Sputnik* in October 1957 engendered a fear of Russian technological superiority. This gave rise to a drive to compete and win the race to space, beginning with better and earlier education.

That sentiment got a boost from the publication of several new books that highlighted the learning potential of young children, and the importance of the early years for mental development. "The most important period for the development of intelligence occurs during the first eight years of life," declared

Benjamin Bloom in 1964 in *Stability and Change in Human Characteristics*.[12] About 50 percent of mental capacity develops between conception and age four and about 80 percent by the age of eight, he wrote. Inspired by these new books, Head Start, the preschool program for disadvantaged children intended to compensate for deficiencies incurred as a result of poor socioeconomic conditions, was established. And this drove middle-class parents to demand a better education for all children.

Shortly thereafter, new research findings appeared, demonstrating that lo and behold preschool children do indeed acquire some reading knowledge with no harmful effect. These findings alleviated parental concerns about early reading development. Fresh studies in the neurosciences were also published, suggesting the existence of sensitive periods in brain development and implying that the early years are a critical period for the development of children's learning potential. All this new information prompted Jeanne Chall, the noted Harvard University reading specialist, to declare in 1977, "The earlier the start, the better."[13]

EMERGENT LITERACY

As evidence from research was accumulating, showing that literacy starts to develop a long time before formal schooling, a new concept began to emerge among reading researchers: emergent literacy. First used by Marie Clay in 1966, this concept took hold in the 1980s. And while current researchers are not unified in their perspectives to studying early literacy, emergent literacy has a number of key tenets. These have been elegantly summarized by David Yaden, Deborah Rowe, and Laurie MacGillivrary:

a. Emergent literacy is concerned with children from birth through kindergarten.
b. This concept deals with reading and writing knowledge as it moves from the unconventional to the conventional (i.e., from pre-reading knowledge to actual reading, from pre-writing marks to real writing).

c. Emergent literacy views children as constructors of
   their own literacy knowledge.
d. Emergent literacy occurs informally.[14]

Let us take a closer look.

Emergent literacy takes an opposite position to the concept
of reading readiness. Instead of having to reach a certain mental
age, or maturation, before children can start learning to read,
emergent literacy argues that in a literate society (including
inner-city neighborhoods) children begin to acquire literacy, informally, from year one. This informal development occurs as
children are engaged in routine daily activities, typical of the
preschool age. As Frank Smith, one of the pioneers in the emergent literacy camp wrote, "Children probably begin to read from
the moment they become aware of print in any meaningful way
. . . the roots of reading are discernible whenever children strive
to make sense of print before they are able to recognize many of
the actual words."[15]

William Teale and Elizabeth Sulzby, other key contributors
to the emergent literacy camp, explained, "We use *emergent* to
suggest that development is taking place, that there is something
new emerging in the child that had not 'been' there before.
Growth in writing and reading comes from within the child and
as the result of environmental stimulation."[16]

Reading and writing knowledge, according to the emergent
literacy perspective, emerge from children's daily interactions
with print in their environment. They learn from their interactions with picture books, storybook readings, reading toys, and
advertisements in newspapers or on television. They learn about
reading and writing from their dramatic plays, cereal boxes, alphabet letters, road signs, storefront names, shopping lists, television guide, postcards from Grandma, restaurant menus, and
so on. Children learn informally to recognize the letters and
memorize some printed words. They learn from which side to
open a book for reading and how to pretend to read from it.

These reading-related interactions occur spontaneously in
most American homes, irrespective of cultural or socioeconomic
background, because nowadays every home is using a variety of
printed materials. Parents and other able readers who interact
with the children provide necessary stimulation, feedback, and

support. And this attention encourages children's literacy development. The more stimulation and encouragement children receive, the more reading and writing development will take place. Emergent literacy is child-centered, accepting children at whatever level they are functioning at, explains Lesley M. Morrow, an early literacy expert.[17] And it is also sensitive to cultural diversity because children can acquire literacy skills also when studying themes that focus on their particular heritage, she adds. (It is interesting to note the similarity between the contemporary emergent literacy perspective and Huey's view on children's reading development articulated in 1908.)

CAPABLE READERS BEFORE AGE SIX

While keeping in mind the emergent literacy perspective, let us sidestep and take a closer look at a subgroup of children who present a growing phenomenon. An increasing number of preschool children become fluent readers before formal schooling without ever being formally taught to read. While most American youngsters today begin to develop their literacy in the preschool years, some three- and four-year olds become fluent readers. It is worthwhile to take a careful look at these children and gain insight that could apply to all children.

Who are these early readers? And how many children can actually read before age six? We have no updated figures. But studies from the 1960s[18] and 1970s[19] concluded that between 1 percent and 3 percent of American children know how to read when they enter kindergarten. These may appear to be small numbers, but actually they are not so small when we realize that it involves more than two hundred thousand children per year. (There are about 12 million children between ages three and five in the United States. Two percent of that is 240,000 children per year.) One can reasonably assume that this number, as impressive as it was, is even higher today, since contemporary parents are more supportive of early literacy development compared to parents of previous generations. They are no longer apprehensive about an early start, realizing the benefits of early reading development. Moreover, educational television programs and literacy-oriented computer software developed since the 1960s and the increasingly more literacy-friendly preschool environment are undoubtedly contributing to early literacy development and to a higher number of preschool readers.

So, if most American children begin the process of learning to read in their preschool years as emergent literacy research indicates, why don't most children become capable readers before formal schooling? We know that this has nothing to do with a high IQ level. It was commonly assumed, during the heyday of the reading readiness concept, that early readers have a higher than average IQ. But we now know that IQ is not a precondition for early reading ability. While it is true that the majority of early readers have a higher-than-average IQ, studies document cases of preschoolers with IQs of less than 100 who also knew how to read. And it may actually be the other way around: the process of early reading development may, in effect, raise children's IQs.

Socioeconomic background, like IQ, is also not a dominant factor in early reading ability. While early readers on the average come from higher socioeconomic levels, they are also found in low socioeconomic families. Yaden, Rowe, and MacGillivrary concluded that "[s]imple explanations such as socioeconomic status are no longer acceptable for explaining a child's literacy failure or success."[20]

There is no agreement among researchers about the association between a child's personality traits and early reading ability. While some investigators found no difference in the characteristics of early readers and matched nonreaders, others report that early readers perform better on certain visual memory and visual discrimination tests. There is also some indication that early readers may be superior in certain auditory tests. And, not surprisingly, there seems to be a strong association between reading and oral language development. Early readers score higher on language screening tests compared to children who are not reading early.

NATURAL READING DEVELOPMENT

The most distinguishing difference between early readers and children who do not read early appears to involve the parents. Increasingly, the focus of attention has shifted to parents and home environment. Numerous studies confirm that these two factors play a crucial role in early reading development.[21] Early readers appear to have homes filled with books and other literacy-related toys and materials, as well as parents who enjoy extensive interactions with their youngsters: discussing, naming, reading, stimulating, and responding to myriad literacy-related and other kinds of questions.

And while many researchers since the 1980s have tried to find out exactly how these children acquire their ability and what the actual learning process they experience is,[22] only one study succeeded to fully uncover the whole process.[23] This study identified the full sequence of that development, the step-by-step process as the children moved from being nonreaders to becoming fluent capable readers.

The next chapters will highlight this process. I will demonstrate its sequence, at what age it starts, how long it lasts, and what facilitates it. I will also discuss whether all children could experience this process of development. But before we can begin this illustration, I need to clarify a term intermittently used in the past few decades in conjunction with preschool readers who were never formally taught to read. I am referring to the term *natural readers* or *natural reading development*. What exactly does this mean?

A number of researchers have suggested that learning to read is a natural process in a literate society, one that does not require formal instruction in its beginning phases.[24] Some suggested that the process of learning to read is similar to the process of learning to speak.[25] "We believe that the great majority of boys and girls can learn to read and write as easily and as naturally as they have learned to talk," write Margaret Jewell and Miles V. Zintz.[26] "Because many children come to school already reading and writing, apparently without formal instruction. . . . Such children were said to have 'learned to read naturally,' a phrase that suggests that their ability to read developed similarly to their acquisition of language or their learning to walk," writes Lesley M. Morrow.[27]

I have adopted this term. Natural readers is a good descriptor of preschool children who become fluent readers with no formal instruction. As a mother of one four-year-old reader explained to me, "His reading was there, it was just a matter of bringing it out." This phrase is also in line with the emergent literacy perspective. Let us take a closer look.

Natural reading development is a process by which a preschool child acquires fluent reading capability without systematic instruction. It appears to be an innate developmental process neither directed nor guided by parents, teachers, or some standard reading methodology, but, instead, by a process that develops within the child as an internal response to reading-related stimuli in the environment. As mentioned earlier, these stimuli can be found in picture books and advertisements in newspapers or on television and on cereal boxes, toothpaste tubes, and ice cream containers. They can appear on road signs, shopping lists, birthday cards, and restaurant menus, and in storybooks, sociodramatic plays, and many other objects, places, or events in the child's environment that have an element of print in them.

It is the child who determines the focus of interest and the duration and pace of his or her interaction with each of these stimuli. The parents (or other caregivers) provide the necessary stimulation, feedback, and support, which are essential in this informal learning process. Similar to oral language development, the chances for natural reading development to fully evolve—that is, for a child to acquire fluent reading ability before formal schooling—depends on the quality and quantity of literacy interactions that exist between that child and the adults in his or her environment.

Following a succession of playful interactions between the child and these literacy stimuli, over a period of eighteen to twenty-four months, a natural process of reading development emerges. It is a quite logical process that incorporates a number of conceptually distinct stages. Slowly progressing through each of these stages, and mastering one reading concept at a time, the child eventually acquires fluent reading capability.

It is important to emphasize that different children experience a similar sequence of development. This fact may indicate that natural reading development, like speech development, follows a natural predetermined course. I will further elaborate on this point in Chapter 9.

The following chapters describe the natural reading development of six children: three little girls and three little boys ranging in age from two years, nine months to four years, ten months. Their stories are strikingly simple. Many of their biographical anecdotes can be found in the homes of many other preschoolers. Yet these six children acquired fluent reading capability by age four when most children do not. As you read through these accounts, you will understand the secret of their accomplishment.

Following the Bush administration's new reading legislation of No Child Left Behind and Reading First programs, these children's stories are especially important. They provide a model for action for parents and teachers who are often confused by the barrage of contradictory information they receive on the topic of early reading. Theories of learning may change but the natural behavior of children, including natural reading development, in a literate society, is quite firm.

Parents are children's first and most important teachers. They can literally open their children's eyes and minds to the world of print at the most impressionable age, gently stimulating youngsters' natural reading development, from year one, on a one-to-one basis. Preschool teachers, who are now under pressure to develop the literacy of children below kindergarten age, will find in the following chapters invaluable information and good ideas. The discussion of what they should and should not do to promote preschooler's literacy, and guidance they can provide to parents about how to facilitate natural reading development at home will be very useful.

Gerald Coles warns educators in his recent book *Reading the Naked Truth*, to watch out for any "legislation mandating authoritarian and harmful prepackaged reading instruction."[28] The proven, "scientifically based" examples that *The Secret of Natural Readers* offers encourage parents and teachers, and empower them, to try their own mix of literacy activities with their youngsters to stimulate children's natural reading development.

Part II

The Children's Stories

Chapter Three

Three Years Old and Reading

Some parents make sand castles with their children, we made words with him.

—Sean's mother

THE GALLEN FAMILY

We begin our tour of the natural readers' environment with a visit to the Gallen home. Living in a small, comfortable house located in a tree-lined suburban neighborhood, Bob and Nan, with their two children and golden retriever, are a fairly typical middle-class family. Both Bob and Nan grew up in the area and their family is extended, with brothers and sisters and many nephews and nieces all living nearby. Four-year-old Sean is their firstborn child (in Bob's second marriage), and little Emily is three years younger. Bob, forty-six, is a high school graduate, employed as a city firefighter. Nan, thirty-three, has two years of college with experience as a legal secretary. She continued to work part time until Sean was two and a half, fortunate to have the flexibility to arrange her work schedule around Bob's shifts at the station. Since Emily's birth, however, she has been a stay-at-home mom, planning possibly to return to work once both children attend school.

The Gallen home is strikingly cozy. It is warmly decorated with old furniture handed down from various family members and beautiful large plants that add a touch of color and life. A large assortment of memorabilia displayed throughout gives the place a distinct personal flavor. And Molly, the family's large golden retriever often stretched out on the carpet with her wagging tail, adds to the calm, warm ambience. The Gallens are relaxed people. Bob shares child-care responsibilities whenever he is at home, and he spends much time doing a variety of woodworking around the house: adding a deck off the kitchen, building a piece of furniture, and occasionally making a wooden toy for one of the children. While they say that they do not have much time to read books, the Gallens like to relax with a magazine and they have subscriptions to *Time*, *Newsweek*, *Woman's Day*, and *Sports Illustrated*.

A NATURAL EARLY READER

The two children are the center of this family. Emily was usually asleep when I came to interview the parents, but Sean, the natural early reader and the focus of my interest, would let me in the house with his winning smile. He is a handsome, appealing boy with the good looks of his father and the sparkling eyes and smiles of his mother. He is of average height, a little on the chubby side, generally healthy, but with some allergy to cats, feathers, and milk. Apparently he was allergic also to his mother's milk and had to be placed on a special soybean formula.

Sean is very sociable. He loves his sister, according to Nan, with no trace of jealousy, and enjoys reading to her and playing house with her. There are sixteen children on their block, ranging in age from one to seven and the neighborhood is very friendly. The children interact daily, playing active and quiet games, indoors and outdoors. They ride their bikes, have Big Wheel races, and play cops and robbers on the sidewalk. During one of my interview sessions with Nan, for instance, Sean had three friends over for a slumber party, and for a special treat, Nan drove the four children to the fire station to visit Bob at work. Curiously, there is one activity, usually a favorite of most preschoolers, that Sean has never enjoyed, Nan relates. He never liked to play with toy trucks. While other neighborhood children were playing in front of their home with their trucks, Sean would go up and down the street playing with his plastic alphabet letters.

How does he pass the time when not playing with other children? As sociable and active as he is, Sean likes to read and color more than anything else, Nan said. He has enjoyed reading since age two and a half, and "he usually reads or colors himself to sleep," Nan relates. "Reading mellows him down. He relaxes with reading." He is exceptionally artistic, and at four and a half enjoys drawing beautiful realistic pictures. Singing and listening to music (in particular light rock music by singers such as Lionel Richie and Kenny Rogers—the type of music, his parents enjoy—are other favorite pastimes. And then there is television. Like most children, Sean enjoys watching television by himself or with his friends, and contrary to popular opinion about precocious children, he may spend some three to four hours a day on the living room carpet, glued to the screen. Overall, Nan feels that he is an easy child, although she says he has mood swings. He can be very cheerful one moment and moody the next. "He is a whiner," she said, and tends to cry easily. But he is also sensitive, a perfectionist, adaptable, active, dependable, independent, friendly, relaxed, and outgoing, Nan added.

It appears that apart from his early reading ability and advanced drawing skill, Sean is a typical preschooler and not much different from many other well-rounded children of comparable age. There is nothing, on the surface of things, that could explain his natural reading development. So how did Sean become a capable early reader? Why did he learn to read at an age when most children do not? Discounting the unlikely possibility that he simply woke up one day knowing how to read, there must have been some developmental process going on for a considerable length of time. "His reading was there; it was just a matter of bringing it out," his mother explained. Both Bob and Nan maintain that they never intended to teach Sean to read, and that they only encouraged him when his reading interest was evident. Once they noticed that he had some ability, they helped him and kept working with him, they say. "It was like a hobby," Nan explained. "Some parents make

sand castles with their children, we made words with him."
And they, too, were amazed when they first realized Sean's ability to read by himself from a new picture book. "Where did it
come from?" they recall asking each other in wonder. And they
appear sincere in their belief that Sean became an early reader
because of an innate ability.

HOW WELL COULD HE READ?

Before attempting to search deeper for insight into Sean's
reading development, let us first find out how well he could actually read. When I first met Sean, he was four and a half years
old. He was referred to me as an early reader, who was not
taught to read, by professor Richard Salzer, who was studying
early readers at the time at the Early Childhood Research Center, University at Buffalo. Professor Salzer had identified Sean
as a reader at age three years, five months, after giving him an
early reading test he had developed. (In that test children had to
demonstrate the ability to read six unfamiliar sentences and
miscall no more than three of the twenty-four words). Before I
started my own investigation of how Sean became a natural
reader at this tender age, I reassessed his reading proficiency.
He was then four years, six months old. Because of his young
age, I decided on an informal assessment at Sean's home, using
books that were readily available to me at our campus reading
center. To relax him as much as possible during the testing situation (in order to obtain a true picture of his ability), we sat on
the living room sofa. Nan sat close by. Following are a few
examples of this interaction:

> Sean refused to read from the reader I had shown him.
> After giving the book only a brief glance, he turned his
> head away. I then opened the first page of *Cowboy Sam
> and Dandy* by Edna Walker Chandler, a picture storybook
> at the preprimer level. He hesitated at first, and then
> asked me to read to him from it. We agreed to alternate
> our reading. I would read a page and then he was to read
> a page. His reading was slow but fluent, pausing at the
> end of each sentence as if waiting for my comment. I

stopped his reading in that book after six sentences and decided to try more difficult material.

Alternating the pages, we then read several sentences from "Firemen," in *What Do They Do?* by Carla Green, a primer-level book. Again I stopped his reading after six sentences. He was slow but fluent, making only one mistake reading "Zeep! Zeep!" instead of "Zeep! Zoop!" When I pointed out his error and asked him to sound out the word, he read it correctly.

Then he read nine sentences in *Sailor Jack and Bluebell's Dive* by Selma and Jack Wassermann, a first-reader-level book. His reading was slow but fluent with no mistakes. Reading seven sentences from *Titch* by Pat Hutchins, a second-reader-level book, and seven sentences from *Red Fox and His Canoe* by Nathaniel Benchley, another second-reader-level book, he was again slow but fluent, making no mistakes with the printed words but beginning to add the word *the* on several occasions. We did not go further than second-grade level. He appeared to be somewhat tired and was losing interest in the mechanical reading of the testing situation, and I decided to end that procedure. I concluded that at four years, six months Sean was capable of reading material on at least the second-grade level. Three months later, when he was four years, nine months old and came to the campus for another test, I had a second opportunity to observe his reading ability. At that time, he read fluently a long paragraph from the testing material and was able to answer correctly all comprehension questions.

Both Bob and Nan are happy about Sean's early reading ability, considering it to be an asset. As Bob explained, "It is helpful. Gives them a head start. Makes it easier on the student and the teacher if he already knows something." They have only one concern, raised by one of Sean's nursery-school teachers, "What will you do with him?" she asked Nan, implying that Sean might get bored in school in the future. But the parents have faith that things will work out for the better, and they

never considered holding back Sean's reading development for
fear that it may pose some problem in the future.

POSSIBLE REASONS FOR SEAN'S EARLY READING ABILITY

How did Sean become a natural early reader? What is the
secret of his early ability? Could an exceptionally high level of
intelligence be at the root of it? One wonders, being precocious
as he is in reading and drawing, how well he would score on an
intelligence test. As it turned out, his standard score on the
Peabody Picture Vocabulary Test, given to him when he was
four years, seven months, was an unremarkable 113. His score
on the Stanford Binet Intelligence Scale, given to him at the
same age by a trained psychologist, was also 113. Both scores
placed him only a notch above average in his mental abilities
as measured by both of these popular tests. It is possible that
the two particular testing days were bad days for Sean, and
that he would have scored higher on another day. It is also possible that his intelligence continued to develop since then. Indeed, when he was given the Stanford Binet test again in
kindergarten, at age five years, three months, his IQ score was
an impressive 147. One must take into account, however, the
possibility that Sean's early reading development by itself has
affected his mental capacity, making it more acute, and thus
raising his score on the later intelligence test. Recent brain research would support that view. We will never know for sure. It
is the question of the chicken and the egg. In any case, Sean
had a "terrific memory" with good visual perception and an eye
for detail, as Nan recalled.

Could another adult, outside Sean's home, have influenced
his early reading development, perhaps a nursery school
teacher? Indeed, when he was three years old, Sean started
going to a church nursery school. Friends from the neighborhood were going there and his parents thought that he should
have the same experience, so they enrolled him in the program.
His adjustment was smooth, recalled Nan, and his social skills
improved. "He learned how to share," she said. But as far as his
literacy development, although he knew how to read books with
large print when he started that program, no specific reading-

related activities were given to him there. "The program was primarily play-oriented," Nan explained.

Since that church nursery school enrolled only three-year-old children, when Sean was four, his parents enrolled him in a prekindergarten program at the neighborhood school. He enjoyed this setting, his mother recalled, and while there, too, no specific reading-related activities were given, he was never bored. One of Sean's teachers in that program, Mrs. Parker, told me that she had noticed at the start of the school year, in October, that Sean was printing on his paintings and drawings. He was also reading to other children, she said, and "reading enhanced his sociability." Still, nothing was done there to advance Sean's reading or writing ability. That nursery school, like the first one, was oriented primarily toward the social and emotional development of children. Any reading-related progress that was made by Sean at the time occurred at home. But Nan was pleased with his impressive growth in artwork, attributing it to the rich variety of art activities given in that prekindergarten program.

Some parents and educators believe that certain television programs may facilitate children's reading development. Could this have been the case with Sean? Did he learn to read from a particular television program? His exposure to *Sesame Street* did start early, when he was six months old. Nan was working part time then, and Bob, who was taking care of Sean while Nan was at work, started putting him in front of the television screen to watch the program. Nan relates that Sean would often sit in front of the television for a couple of hours a day, looking at the program from time to time and listening to its sounds. She recalls that he liked the voice of Big Bird more than anything else. But she does not think that he got much out of it at that age. From the age of eighteen months until he was three, he continued to watch the program daily, often two or three, times. And even now, at four and a half, he still enjoys watching *Sesame Street* occasionally.

In addition to *Sesame Street*, Sean was permitted to turn on the television whenever he wanted, viewing a variety of programs. This went on until recently when Bob started to encourage him to watch mainly quality programs on PBS. (Father and son often view a good adult program together.) There was also an early period when Sean was attracted to television commercials, the parents recalled. But overall, Nan does not think that Sean's reading development was much affected by watching *Sesame Street* or any of the other programs. We may conclude, therefore, that while it is likely that *Sesame Street* and some other television programs may have contributed to Sean's reading development, these programs were not the decisive factor in his early development. Many preschoolers watch *Sesame Street* and television commercials and they do not become early readers. So there must have been another reason for Sean's early reading development.

SOLVING THE MYSTERY

To fully understand how Sean became a capable early reader, and grasp the forces and events that helped shape his development, it is necessary to step into the daily home environment in which this development took place. Since the learning process was nonsystematic, and to a large extent spontaneous, we can at best take a look at a good-sized sample of the boy's reading-related interactions as they occurred in that environment, and then try to make some sense of these. Let us then look at some key groups of anecdotes, taken from the reconstructed chronicle of Sean's reading development as related by his parents. These accounts describe literacy events from year one to the present. (It is important to keep in mind that many of these anecdotes were embedded in Sean's typical early childhood activities, and were extracted from these for the purpose of the study.)

Sean's First Interactions with Books

Nan recounted that when Sean was about nine months old she started to buy sturdy baby books and cloth books for him to look at. These were mostly farm and ABC books. For his first birthday, Sean received two new books, one about animals and one about numbers. Nan recalls that Sean used to look through these books and often enjoyed listening to his parents read to him from them. But there was nothing unusual about his interest or attitude toward books and reading at the time. He was very much like any other child of similar age in that regard.

The First Encounters with Alphabet Letters

Like many anxious first-time mothers, Nan would often compare her son's development with that of other children of similar age. Is he slower? Is he faster? Is his mental development all right? When he was one year old, she happened to observe a child of a friend, of similar age, who was able to identify letters and numbers. Nan was so impressed by that child's ability that she began to wonder if letter and number identification was a developmental expectation for one-year-old children. And she wondered why Sean did not have that ability. Determined that he would not lag behind others, she set out to buy colorful magnetic letters for him, to stimulate the development of his letter knowledge.

From then on, Bob and Nan started casually playing (working) with Sean with these letters. For example, they would show him a letter, saying, "Here is a B. Here is a C." and ask him to repeat the letter's name. They also used to spell his name with the letters. Sean liked these magnetic letters (Nan recalled how he often used to bite on them), and he enjoyed playing with them with his parents—on the floor, on the kitchen table, or on the refrigerator door. But there was no indication at the time that the letters had any special significance for him, Nan recounted. Casually, Bob and Nan continued to play with him with those letters, not thinking much about it. They considered it just another manifestation of good parenting—stimulating Sean's print awareness just as much as they stimulated other aspects of his growth.

An Attraction to Television Commercials

There was one print-related activity that did excite Sean at age one, recalled Nan, and that was television commercials. He would be drawn to the room whenever a commercial would flash on the television screen. Bob recalled that "I'm a Pepper, you're a Pepper" and another soft-drink commercial were two of Sean's favorites around that age. (It may be that these were some of his parents' favorite drinks.) At first, he was amused by these commercials; by eighteen months, he started to repeat words from them; and then, somewhat later, he began to sing them. At two, Sean would recognize words from television commercials on merchandise in the supermarket, Bob and Nan related.

The nonsystematic, spontaneous, and playful interactions with the letters, and the excitement over familiar words on television commercials and supermarket merchandise, continued throughout the following months. And for Christmas Sean received another set of magnetic letters to accommodate his many letter activities. In the meantime, he learned the order of the alphabet and enjoyed lining up the letters in order. Often, when his mother would be working in the kitchen, Sean would play near her, alphabetically arranging the colorful magnetic letters on the refrigerator door.

And then, at eighteen months, there was a burst of excitement in the Gallen home. As if overnight, Sean's potential for early reading began to manifest itself, and the parents recall that period as a landmark. It was actually Grandma who first noticed Sean's ability and made the parents aware of it. She was babysitting Sean and was caught by surprise one day when she noticed that he could read the numbers and letters on her knitting instructions. Busy making an afghan with letters on it for him, she observed that he could name correctly any letter on the afghan. While it had been known in the family that Sean could identify his magnetic letters, no one had expected him at that age to be able to identify *any* letter at random. His grandmother was so impressed that she bought a large set of letters for Sean to play with at her home. It would be a good way to keep him busy while she was working on the afghan, she thought.

An Obsession with Letters

Overnight, Sean became "really obsessed with letters." He started to see letters everywhere and in everything. For instance, the cross on church steeples started to look to him like the letter *T;* the broken yellow dividing line along the streets became many

*I*s in his eyes; tree branches appeared to have many *Y*s; and so on. The Gallens could not explain this burst of association with the letters, and they are unaware of having done anything in particular to encourage in Sean this strong preoccupation with letters. "He may have seen it on *Sesame Street*, Nan reflected, where letter associations are projected in many segments. But she is more inclined to believe that this intense interest was driven by something internal to Sean. (It is important to keep in mind the possibility that the excitement engendered around him by his letter knowledge may have further stimulated Sean to an even greater awareness of the letters, and so attract even more positive feedback from the people around him.)

Sean's obsession with letters manifested itself also in other ways, as for example, in the choice of a babysitter. His favorite babysitter at that time was a high school girl, an avid gymnast, who was able to do the shapes of the letters with her body. She loved to pose the letters for him, and with every letter she made, she would ask Sean, "What's this?" and he would name the letter for her. Both Sean and his sitter enjoyed so much those playful interactions that she started bringing her friends along to the Gallen home to show off to them little Sean's ability to identify the letters she was posing for him. And a sister of that sitter, a student teacher at the time, was so impressed that she took Sean to her school to demonstrate his ability to her fellow students. "It was like Show and Tell," Nan reflected, and "Sean enjoyed being shown off."

The First Words

Deciding to be supportive of Sean's intense interest in the letters, the Gallens bought him a special backpack in which to keep his letters. "Letters were like friends to him," Nan recounted. And he would carry them along whenever they would go to visit friends. During the same period, in parallel to his intense interest in letters, the Gallens noticed that Sean began to focus on printed words. His attention would be drawn to individual letters as well as to certain whole words. They vividly recall that by eighteen months Sean could read words such as *stop* and *go*. To prove the point, Nan related an anecdote involving a trip to Florida in which they told relatives about Sean's ability to read words. An aunt started arguing that this could not be real "reading" and that Sean had probably memorized the words by the shapes of the signs. To demonstrate to her that she and the other relatives were wrong, that Sean could actually read those words, Nan wrote *stop* and *go* on a piece of paper and asked Sean to read those words. He did, and the relatives were impressed.

If traffic sign words were among the first words Sean could recognize by sight (he probably learned these words during walks around the neighborhood and on car rides), storefront names were soon to follow. "What's the name of this store?" one of his parents would ask, pointing at the store's name, or, "Look, here is . . ." His interest in books also became more intense at that period, and increasingly, Sean would ask his parents to read to him, paying careful attention to the story line. Being sensitive to his interests and responses, the Gallens started reading to him daily. He enjoyed that, in particular at bedtime, they recalled.

The days rolled by peacefully at the Gallen household, and Sean's interest in letters and words increasingly attracted the attention of other family members and friends. They started giving him reading-related gifts on different occasions: alphabet blocks, more magnetic letters with boards, a variety of alphabet flash cards, and the like. Nan recalled that he enjoyed in particular to play with one set of cards that had uppercase letters on one side and lowercase letters on the other. Another set of cards he often played with had a capital letter with its corresponding small letter and a picture of a word beginning with that letter on one side, with a list of four words—three starting with the featured letter and one, for contrast, with a different letter—on the other side. For example, if the featured letter was *D* with a picture of a dog, the words *Dick, Doll, Bell, Dog*, for instance, would be listed on the other side of that card. At age two he could read by sight words such as *Stop, Go, On, Off, Shoe, Dog, and Cat*, recalled the parents.

Favorite Word Games

And what about writing? Many children show an interest in writing simultaneously with a desire for reading. Was that the case with Sean? His curiosity about writing slowly became apparent to his parents but only after he was able to recognize a number of words, they say. Once he understood that there is a connection between letters and words, that is, that words are in fact constructed with letters, he became intrigued with how words are put together. And it became a kind of a game for him, a riddle, and a challenge. But lacking, at age two, the fine finger dexterity to write in any conventional manner (this is a later development), he started to put words together with his letter cards, letter blocks, or magnetic letters; simple words that were meaningful to him, such as *Sean, Mom, Dad, Nan, Bob*, and *Emily*.

How would you react had your preschooler struggled to put a word together with magnetic letters? Bob, who first noticed Sean's attempts, was eager to help. At first he would simply show him the spelling of the particular word and let the boy copy his example. Then he started playfully to work with Sean on the sounds of the letters, thinking that if Sean knew the letters' sounds, he would be able to form most words by himself rather than ask his parents for help. Casually, Bob started to play letter and sound games with Sean to help his learning. For example, Sean would take a small familiar word such as *at* and try to add different letters to it, to form a new word such as *bat, fat*, or *cat*. The father would take an *S* and put it in front of the word *top* to show Sean the new word *Stop*. Or, one of the parents would take a word such as *top* and ask Sean, "What letter could you change that would make a new word?" and he would spell *pop* or *hop*. They did similar things with words such as *pig, dig*, and *fig* or *hot, tot*, and *cot*. "These were games to him," Nan explained, "he enjoyed playing them," spending concentrated periods of time on the carpet or standing by the refrigerator door playing these word games.

There is no doubt that Bob and Nan enjoyed their reading-related interactions with their son. Although he had an active life, filled with many activities that are typical of the preschool years—with literacy being only one among many other areas of growth—the Gallens considered reading to be a key to Sean's mental development. Intuitively, they had a tremendous respect for that aspect of his growth. And they had no inhibition to help him, from an early age, whenever they thought he was ready to learn something in that domain. So, they stimulated Sean's print awareness in addition to his speech development, social development, artistic development, and physical development. At thirty months, he was so eager to learn to spell out words that whenever someone would come to the house Sean would draft him for that activity. "What's his name?" he would ask. "How do you spell it?" Once the visitor's name was spelled out for him, Sean would arrange the corresponding letters on the floor or on the refrigerator door. Often he would have a word spelled for him on a sheet of paper and then study it carefully, Nan recalled.

And then a new spurt of development occurred. Around the age of thirty months, Sean started to pick up picture books, that had been read to him before, to read aloud by himself. His pronunciations were very clear, Nan recalled, and he could easily read three- and four-letter words. She would test him, from time to time, curious to find out if he was actually reading the text or just recalling from memory—purposely making a few errors to see if he would notice. But she could never fool him. Sean could always detect any error she had made, and promptly corrected her. Somewhat later, when he started to read unfamiliar books by himself and would come across a short, unfamiliar word, he would try to sound out the word, but when encountering a long unfamiliar word, he would ask one of his parents for help. They would sound out the word for him and he would repeat it after them.

Going to the Public Library

Preschool children love to go to the public library. They feel so grown up. Once Nan noticed Sean's growing enjoyment in picture books, she started taking him to the public library, and let him select a book or two by himself. The Gallens also started to order books by mail for Sean, selecting from the recommended titles in *Sesame Street* magazine, to which they had a subscription. *The Shape of Me and Other Stuff* and *The Cat in The Hat* by Dr. Seuss, and *Hand, Hand, Fingers, Thumbs* by Al Perkins were the first three books they ordered specially for him through the mail. Another special order, arriving a few months later, included *The Foot Book* and *One Fish, Two Fish, Red Fish, Blue Fish* by Dr. Seuss; *The Bears' Picnic* by Stan and Jan Berenstain; and *Babar Loses His Crown* by Laurent De Brunhoff. Sean loved to receive these special packages addressed to him and would excitedly tear off their wrapping. During that period, around thirty months, he also started to write with a pencil, gradually developing the fine finger dexterity needed for writing with a conventional writing instrument. He had an excellent visual memory for letters and numbers, Nan recalled, relating another anecdote from a trip to Florida: as she was writing postcards to send to friends back home, she was stunned when Sean was able to tell her their friends' house number.

Yet books and letter-and-word games were not the only reading sources for Sean. A variety of printed materials would continuously and spontaneously provide an impetus for reading events, at home as well as outside. Food containers in the supermarket, for example, were an easily available source of reading. Sean would recognize familiar words from *Sesame Street* or television commercials and excitedly read them to his parents. Or Bob and Nan would point at a word they thought would be of interest to him, and read it for him. "Look, here is . . ." they would say, with Sean repeating the word after them. *Orange, milk,* and *apple* were some of the first words he could read in the supermarket, at age thirty months. Once he knew how to read *ice cream,* he started to sound out flavor words such as *strawberry* and *chocolate.*

The refrigerator door in the Gallen home was always covered with colorful magnetic letters, and Sean could readily see what happened to a word when one of its letters was exchanged. Around age three, he knew, for example, that words such as *Mom, Dad, Bob,* and *Nan* are the same even if spelled backwards. He knew that *Molly,* the name of the family dog—one of his first sight vocabulary words—could be changed into *Mommy,* when you take out the *L*s and replace them with *M*s. At that time, he also received a blackboard for chalking, and he printed on it words (in uppercase) that were close to his heart: *Sean, Mom, Dad,* and *Molly,* for example, the same words he used to put together with his magnetic letters on the refrigerator door.

FAMOUS SEAN

On his third birthday, Sean could read by himself cards given to him by relatives and friends. One of his favorite gifts on that occasion was a set of *Sesame Street* cards that had cutout words with small letters to fill in the cut spaces. These cards were helpful for building his reading vocabulary, Nan explained. He used them to practice putting words together. He also received two T-shirts from neighbors, reflecting his social standing in that neighborhood; one shirt had ALPHA BOY printed on it, and the other FAMOUS SEAN. He was the wunderkind among his relatives and friends, the child who knew how to read before formal schooling. "He could spell the word *elephant* on the refrigerator door," exclaimed to me one of Nan's friends during one of my visits to the Gallen's home. "He could also spell the word *Greg* [the name of that friend's husband]," she remarked in amazement.

A few additional anecdotes are worth relating. When Sean was about three and a half, and already able to easily read picture books by himself, Nan bought him the *Sesame Street Dictionary*, and he enjoyed reading words from it. This may seem somewhat perplexing because there is no story line to follow in a dictionary to keep one's interest, so why would a capable reader be interested in reading a dictionary? Yet the fact is that many preschoolers enjoy picture dictionaries, possibly because they can better understand the meaning of the words from the corresponding illustrations. It is also possible that when they do not have to pay attention to the content of a story, they can better focus on the form of the words, and the mechanics of the reading process, an activity that they may intuitively find useful for their reading development.

From time to time, Nan would also buy a workbook for Sean from the corner drugstore, their favorite toy store, or, occasionally, the supermarket. Oblivious to the fact that commercial workbooks are often judged by early childhood educators to be too structured and to restrict a child's imagination, she bought him a "Count and Color" workbook, an "Addition and Subtraction" workbook, and plain coloring books with a few sentences per page. Sean loved working in these books. He liked to complete the dot-to-dot pictures and follow the written directions, Nan recalled.

Words kept fascinating Sean. On one occasion, for example, he discovered that certain words have smaller words inside them: *top* inside *stop*, *pen* inside *open*, *all* inside *small*, and so on. And so, between age three and a half and four, he would play word-detection games with his parents, searching for small words inside larger ones. It was a mental game for him, recalled the Gallens. They also played a vowel-hunting game after Bob had explained to Sean that most words have a vowel.

At four years, six months old, Sean still loved to listen to his parents read to him. Sitting on his father's lap in one of the living room's comfortable armchairs, or huddled together at the kitchen table, Bob worked with him every day. Nan would also spend some time reading with Sean daily. But now, it was mostly Sean who would read aloud to his parents. His reading ability continued to aid him socially, Nan related, and he continued to be a popular boy. Neighborhood children, who were in the first and second grades, would test his reading ability from time to time, but these were his friends, Nan explained, and he got tremendous satisfaction when they were impressed with his reading and coloring skills, especially when they would let out an impressive "Wow!" she added.

SO HOW DID SEAN LEARN TO READ?

Although Bob and Nan honestly maintain that they did not teach Sean to read and that he would have become an early reader in any home environment because of an innate ability, it is obvious that a great deal of incidental learning and teaching did occur in the Gallen home. But because they never *intended* to teach Sean, and they had no systematic plan for their reading-related interactions with him—primarily stimulating his print awareness and responding to his reading-related interests and queries—they never considered these interactions to be formal instruction. In their minds it was plain good parenting: a sense of responsibility to encourage Sean's literacy development just as they encouraged all the other aspects of his growth. Reading-related events happened in the Gallen family naturally, in the context of daily life activities. It was as natural as Sean's speech development, social development, and physical development.

Following a careful analysis of Sean's reading behavior it became clear that he did experience a lengthy learning process before becoming a capable reader, a process that stretched over a period of some twenty months—from the age of eighteen months until he was about three years old. However, since nothing was planned or fully thought out, the interesting question is whether Sean's reading development involved a random process, or a logical sequence of growth. As it turned out, the analysis of the data revealed an interesting pattern, one based on several distinct stages or phases of growth:

1. It appears that Sean, like most children, first experienced a preliminary period in which he gained general knowledge about books and print. That period, which started in his first year of life, included exposure to *Sesame Street*, interactions with picture books, attraction to television commercials, playing with colorful letter blocks, his parents readings to him, and so forth. But until he was about eighteen months old, there was nothing noteworthy about his reading development. He was very much like many other children of comparable age.

2. At eighteen months, some change occurred. It was as if Sean's mind began to open up to reading-related events and he started to connect with print, mentally and emotionally, absorbing whatever the environment had to offer. His reading behavior began to accelerate. He became obsessed with letters and shortly thereafter mastered the alphabet. Simultaneously, he began to recognize a growing list of words—storefront names, direction words, and other words that were especially meaningful to him. He also began to be passionate about picture books. This intense interest in print, which included many letter games, lasted for a period of about six months.

3. At twenty-four months, a new conceptual development occurred. While he continued to be interested in the letters and in a growing list of printed words, Sean also developed a strong interest in making words. And he started to spend concentrated periods of time on forming words with his magnetic letters and his letter cards. This was an important step from the standpoint of his cognitive development, because the ability to put together words with magnetic letters shows that

he began to understand that words are made from letters, and he wanted to experiment with that idea. This
was, in fact, a form of emergent writing, but not yet
having the fine finger dexterity and eye/hand coordination necessary for writing with a pencil or any other
conventional writing utensil (which usually develops
later), he made words with his colorful magnetic letters. At the same time that his interest in forming
words was evident (and probably because of that),
Bob started to play letter-sound games with Sean, intuitively trying to help him with his word activities.

4. Again, about a half year later, around the age of thirty
   months, another step of progress occurred. While continuing to improve his reading-related knowledge—
   increasing the number of words he could recognize
   and advancing his ability to form words—Sean now
   began to read familiar books by himself. Often he
   would read these books to his parents. He also started
   to sound out short, unfamiliar words.

5. Some six months later, at the age of thirty-six months,
   another spurt of development occurred. Sean started to
   show interest in sounding out long, unfamiliar words.

6. His ability to read easy, unfamiliar books improved
   and his confidence was growing. Slowly, at the age of
   thirty-eight months, Sean was becoming an independent early reader.

This developmental progression can be summarized as follows:

Stage 1: Sean gained general knowledge about books
          and print (starting in his first year).
Stage 2: Sean learned the names of the letters and
          began to recognize printed words (starting at
          eighteen months).
Stage 3: Sean focused on forming words and learn-
          ing the sounds of letters (starting at twenty-four
          months).
Stage 4: Sean enjoyed reading to his parents from fa-
          miliar books and sounding out short, unfamiliar
          words (starting at thirty months).

Stage 5: Sean began to sound out long, unfamiliar
     words (starting at thirty-six months).
Stage 6: Sean began to read easy, unfamiliar books
     (starting at thirty-eight months).

Each of these developmental stages was characterized by a
distinct reading behavior, which engaged Sean for a period of
several months. Each of these stages appeared to be a prerequisite for the following stage, a necessary step in the ladder of the
boy's reading development. It must be noted, however, that the
distinct reading behavior that marked each period did not terminate with the emergence of the new phase. It continued to be
present and evolve throughout the subsequent stages, but it was
no longer of central interest to the child. It is as though Sean had
grasped, while being in each phase, a particular concept that
was necessary for his reading development, and once it was mastered, he moved on. He would continue to use the skill, but it
would no longer be of special interest to him, and he no longer
needed to spend much time, and mental effort, to learn it.

CONCLUSION

One can conclude with a great degree of certainty that Sean
did not learn to read by himself. Although his parents honestly
discount their importance in his reading development, having
followed no systematic method of reading instruction with him,
they did encourage Sean's learning intuitively, in a natural spontaneous manner. They stimulated his print awareness from an
early age, sensitively following his interest and level of ability.
They were impressed and excited about every step of progress
that he made, and they let him know it. They playfully challenged Sean but never pressured him, while he in return loved to
impress them, and worked hard at that. In other words, the Gallens facilitated Sean's reading development naturally. They intuitively brought out the child's reading ability in a similar fashion
to parents who facilitate their children's ability to talk.

Chapter Four

———————

Carrie's Story

At one magical instant in your early childhood, the page of a book—that string of confused, alien ciphers—shivered into meaning. Words spoke to you, gave up their secrets; at that moment, whole universes opened. You became, irrevocably, a reader.

—Alberto Manguel, *A History of Reading*

THE MILLER FAMILY

We continue our tour of natural readers' homes with a visit to the Millers. With both father and mother working full time outside the home, how has this couple managed to facilitate the natural reading development of their daughter Carrie? Are there any similarities between Carrie's and Sean's reading development?

Living in another western New York town (but never having met the Gallens), the Millers own a comfortably furnished stone house, located in a well-kept middle-class neighborhood. The family includes the father, thirty-eight, the mother, thirty-seven, four-year-old Carrie, and her sister, Jenny, who is twenty months younger. Both parents are employed by the local university. Dr. Miller is an associate professor of chemistry; Mrs. Miller is an accountant in one of the academic departments. They were married nine years before starting their family, not ready to have children before that. Mrs. Miller was not sure that she would be a good mother. Both parents are natives of the region. The father, relaxed and laid back, was raised in a small rural town; the mother, somewhat more restless and intense, grew up in the city. They have no relatives in the local area.

Sharing child-care responsibilities, Dr. Miller spends much time with Carrie and Jenny. "He helps much more than the average father," Mrs. Miller acknowledged, "to the point of being discriminated against at work for that," she said. From the moment they get home from work until the girls go to bed, they spend all their time with them. Being only twenty months apart, the girls used to share most home activities, but in recent months, the Millers started to give them individualized attention, to optimize each girl's development. Some thirty to forty-five minutes are devoted to that every evening, alternating their interactions with the girls so that each gets to work with each parent—reading, doing some writing activities, and holding elaborate discussions. They are quite indulgent with the girls, Mrs. Miller admitted, alluding to her "working-mother" guilt feelings, and the two "are not too disciplined therefore," she explained. Still, she feels guilty, in particular toward Carrie, because "Carrie is a much more sensitive child than Jenny," and "she needs a very solid home base." She sounded somewhat regretful that her own emotional needs to work prevent her from spending more time with Carrie, and she often worries about her, said Mrs. Miller.

RAISING THEIR NATURAL READER

So how did Carrie become a capable early reader? The parents maintain they had never planned to teach Carrie to read. "I don't think one can teach at this age," Mrs. Miller remarked. "We went along with the child's interests. . . . We encouraged her and did a lot of exposing." She "had a natural inclination to look at patterns, she loved to scan the patterns, and we read to her so much. . . . *Sesame Street* was also helpful in sounding," Dr. Miller added. Both parents believe that Carrie had an innate ability that helped her learn to read early.

A closer look at the Millers' home environment provides some insight into Carrie's development. Although they waited nine years to start their family, once Carrie was born things were thrown into such disarray at the Miller's household that the child virtually began her life in an office. Initially, Mrs. Miller had planned to take the summer off and stay home with Carrie for a few months, but her work at the office turned out to be indispensable, and she was forced to return sooner than planned. Since no suitable child-care provision had been arranged at that point, and with no relatives in the area to help, Mrs. Miller took the baby along to her office. Carrie was then three weeks old. And for the next four months, the mother's office is where she spent her days.

At first the Millers considered placing Carrie in a day-care facility. They looked into some ten possible centers, and found them all to be "awful," providing an undesirable environment for a growing baby. Having met a British woman in her late fifties who was willing to come to the house daily to help them take care of Carrie, they hired her as a nanny. And so, from the time she was four months old until age three when she started going to nursery school, Carrie spent her weekdays with Mrs. Baker. When Jenny was born, Mrs. Baker took care of both girls, and she still helps out with them twice a week. "The girls think she is the greatest person," Mrs. Miller recounted.

But Carrie was a difficult child for the Millers. It may have been her personality or their lack of readiness for parenting, they explain, but although she was a full-term baby with overall good health, they found her demanding. She needed little sleep and cried a lot, also at night. While still in the hospital, when other babies would fall asleep after nursing, Carrie would stay fully awake and cry. In hindsight, Dr. Miller thinks she may have been simply hungry. Breast-fed until she was ten months old, she probably was not fed enough, he said, and that's why she cried so much. Mrs. Miller reflected that Carrie's restlessness may have stemmed from their own (the parents') nervousness about having a first child at her advanced age of thirty-seven. Knowing that a first pregnancy later in life has a greater chance to produce a problematic child, she was continually apprehensive about a potential problem.

Luckily, the Millers found two ways that would calm Carrie in those early months. She would stop crying whenever one of them would talk to her or read aloud in her proximity. It did not matter what they were saying or what they were reading as long as she heard their voices. Since there was not much to talk to her about in those early days, the parents started reading aloud technical, work-related material near Carrie. This would calm her and it "helped our own survival," Mrs. Miller recalled. Moreover, having heard that early exposure to reading could facilitate a child's mental development, they were more than happy to read to her a lot.

So aside from its soothing effect, how has this early exposure to reading affected Carrie? It came across clearly in my long interviews with the Millers that reading was a lifeline between Carrie and her parents, from the very beginning. And soon it would become Carrie's favorite activity. She has been surrounded by books, at home and in the car, from an early age, and has become attached to them. At first she would look at the pictures, then she began to pretend to read, and now that she knows how to read, she likes to show off her ability, explained her mother. She likes to sit at her child-size table in the kitchen, and read aloud while her mother prepares supper. Often she would entertain the family after supper, reading to them.

Yet, as precocious as she is in her reading development, Carrie is still very limited in her social interactions, according to her parents. Slim, fine featured, with smooth dark hair and large blue eyes, she is, at four years, ten months, somewhat tense and withdrawn. A school photo that shows her tensely smiling and with two clenched fists "is a typical portrayal," Mrs. Miller remarked. "She was born with a frown on her face and big open eyes, as if trying from the start to figure things out," Dr. Miller recounted. "Carrie got all the bad qualities and Jenny got all the good qualities," the mother further reflected, chuckling. She interacts primarily with Jenny, enjoying to play "pretend" games with her—acting out favorite stories such as *The Three Bears* and *The Three Little Pigs*, or dramatizing "hospital" scenes following their nanny's accident and hospitalization event.

HOW WELL COULD CARRIE READ?

What was Carrie's actual reading ability? When I first met her, she was four years, ten months old, having just recently been identified as a reader at the Early Childhood Research Center at the University at Buffalo. Curious to find out the extent of her ability, I made my own informal assessment. (This time it was carried out on campus rather than at home because this was more convenient for the parents.) Following are some examples from that interaction:

> Carrie entered the room with her mother and sister. Directly approaching my table, she seated herself on a chair facing me. It was late in the afternoon, at the end of a long day at nursery school, and she seemed a bit tired. I offered Mrs. Miller a chair next to Carrie, but she declined, suggesting that it would be better if she stayed out of the room. She told Carrie that she would be all right, and left. Carrie started to show me the two dinosaur books she had brought along with her. I made a few comments, and then showed her the book with the six sentences. She read these right away, fluently, without a single mistake, and I continued with selections from the Macmillan Basal Readers. Her reading in this series, overall, was rapid in a barely audible voice.
>
> She read three pages (thirteen sentences) from the story "Mouse Wants a Friend" by Helen Piers in the primer-level book, making no mistakes. She then read two pages (six long sentences) fluently with no errors from the story "Little Blue and Little Yellow" by Leo Lionni in the First Reader.
>
> She read six long sentences from "What's Fun without a Friend" by Chihiro Iwasaki in the Second Reader. She made no errors in the words she was reading but skipped a line. I thought that she was getting tired.
>
> Still, she continued to read five long sentences from "Max" by Rachel Isadora in the Third Reader. She was reading the sentences fluently, making no mistakes in the printed words, but beginning to add, omit, and substitute some words. For instance, adding *he* in one sentence, substituting *at* for *in* in another sentence, or omitting *the* and *Lisa*, in two other sentences.

My questions following each reading selection indicated Carrie had a good grasp of the material she was reading and I decided to stop my assessment at that point. I concluded that Carrie had the technical ability to read at least at the third-grade level.

HOW DID SHE DO IT?

As mentioned earlier, the Millers considered reading to be a highly valued activity, and they assigned it a special role in Carrie's life from day one. It was their most reliable means to calm Carrie, a way to develop her mental ability, in addition to being a cherished pastime to compensate for Mrs. Miller's working-mother guilt feelings. Carrie received so much adult attention around reading that it soon became her shining activity—a source of affirmation, identity, and personal strength. While no one had intended to teach her to read, and no one had taken the full responsibility for teaching her, many teaching moments did occur in Carrie's life, spontaneously and naturally, day in and day out.

A closer look at anecdotes related by the Millers illustrates Carrie's reading development from early on. They recall that whenever she would cry, one of them would hold Carrie and read to her. Being their first child, and feeling guilty about leaving her with a nanny, they took turns staying up with her at night, reading to her as long as she was crying. At first they read primarily from their professional material. She was attracted to their voices and to their attention, they explained, rather than to the content of the text, so it did not matter to her what they were reading. And they found these readings to be highly effective. Within a few months, the father noticed that Carrie was scanning geometric patterns on the liner in the crib, and she began to observe patterns on her sheets and her parents' shirts and blouses. Soon, she would trace the patterns with her finger, the mother recalled.

Nursery Books

When she was three months old, her parents started to read to her from nursery books. They noticed that she was beginning to understand, and the content started to matter, so they bought her first children's book, a beautifully produced *Best Mother Goose Ever* by Richard Scarry. They read rhymes to her from this book every day, over and over again, while holding her on their laps. She was listening intently, Mrs. Miller recalled. At four months, she started rocking to the rhythm of "Barber, Barber, Shave a Kid," one of her favorites in *Best Mother Goose Ever*, Dr. Miller related.

Impressed with Carrie's early attention to print, they recalled an episode that occurred at the supermarket, when she was about six months old. Carrie was sitting in her carriage holding the store's advertising paper and pretending to read it, when several shoppers stopped to comment, "Look, the baby is reading." "She always held reading material in the right position," Mrs. Miller commented. And "she always leafed through books one page at a time," Dr. Miller added.

Soon, family members would begin to respond to Carrie's interest in print. One aunt, for example, gave her an old set of wooden alphabet blocks that had belonged to Carrie's mother and her grandmother years ago. She enjoyed playing with the blocks in her playpen. Months later, these old blocks would be used to teach Carrie the letters.

In addition to the rhymes from *Best Mother Goose Ever*, the Millers started reading to Carrie from other sturdy picture books that had information about daily life. And they ordered several books through the mail. Before she was one year old, Carrie received *Sharing*, *You Do It Too*, and *Bathtime*, all Brimax Books, and *My House*, *Words*, and *What Animals Do*, all Golden Books. All these were easy picture books with just a few words per page and the Millers used these books to interact with Carrie. She loved to snuggle on their laps while they were reading. "Maybe that's why she learned to read early," her mother reflected. At seven months, they bought her *I Am a Bunny* by Ole Rison, an exceptionally beautifully illustrated picture book, with a single sentence per page. They had to read her that book daily, over and over. "Where is the butterfly?" "Where is the yellow flower?" the father would ask Carrie before she could even talk, waiting for her to point to the correct illustration. The nanny also used to read a lot to Carrie at the time, making a point of talking to her about the pictures. Soon Carrie could point to the illustrations on request, recalled Dr. Miller. Months later, when Carrie started to talk, she knew *I Am a Bunny* by heart. She still likes that book, related Mrs. Miller, and she now enjoys reading it to her sister.

By the time she was one year old, "Carrie was established in the family as a book nut." For her first birthday, an aunt gave her a copy of *The Runaway Bunny* by Margaret Brown, and another relative gave her a copy of *Goodnight Moon* by the same author. The father, mother, and nanny would now have to read to Carrie daily from these books. She became so attached to them that she started "reading" even in the car, while riding from one place to another, Mrs. Miller recounted.

Pointing Out Words

During her second year, Carrie started to recognize words. These were at first names of local stores, and direction words such as *exit, in, out, push, pull, stop,* and *go.* She picked up these words during walks in the neighborhood. "We took a lot of walks before Jenny was born," Mrs. Miller recounted. And she learned words during shopping trips. "I would point at sign words and read them to her," the mother explained, "or we would rhetorically ask her, 'Where are we now, Carrie?' pointing at a store's name, and then say 'We are at——, or——.'" Once inside a store, direction words provided another source for sight vocabulary. When Carrie was about a year and a half, Mrs. Baker, the nanny, decided to encourage her letter knowledge, in parallel to building up her sight vocabulary. At first she used the old letter blocks as an aid, recalled the Millers. Once Carrie could recognize the letters by their names, Mrs. Baker began to slowly introduce the sounds of the letters. All this was done casually during playful game time.

When Carrie was eighteen months old, her maternal grandmother gave her a copy of *Gingerbread Man* by Arno. She developed a special attachment to that character and the book would turn out to be such a favorite and be used so extensively that several copies had to be purchased for her. Even the cakes for her second and third birthdays had to be made in the shape of the Gingerbread Man. That grandmother was especially sensitive to Carrie's reading development, and shortly before Jenny was born, she started mailing Carrie cards for reading. On each card she would print a few words, thinking, "this would help Carrie's reading," in addition to providing an interesting way to communicate with an out-of-town grandchild. Carrie cherished those cards, and she saved them in a special drawer, spreading them out occasionally on her bed to enjoy the pictures. Twice a month, these cards would arrive, until grandmother and granddaughter started writing letters to each other.

A Subscription to a Book Club

Carrie's ability to recognize isolated words slowly expanded, and the Millers, who were excited about it, decided to reward her with a subscription to the Sesame Street Book Club. She was twenty months old at the time, and the books, which were addressed to Carrie, started arriving by mail, two at a time. Some fifteen books appeared at the house that way, and Carrie was very happy and proud about each arrival, her mother recounted.

By the time she was two, Carrie could look at newspapers and magazines and pick out familiar words such as *green beans* and *baby*, and names of local stores, Mrs. Miller recalled. By then, she had also memorized *Gingerbread Man*, and often pretended to read it. Most importantly perhaps, she proudly started going to the public library checking out a book or two each time.

Some may say at this point that Carrie must have had an exceptionally high level of intelligence to be able to recognize all these words, and that is why she learned to read early. This is true. She did get a good score on two standard intelligence tests—her score on the Peabody Picture Vocabulary Test, given when she was four years, eleven months, was 139, placing her in the ninety-ninth percentile. Her IQ score on the Stanford Binet Intelligence Scale administered at the same age was 115, placing her in the eighty-third percentile. Furthermore, it turned out that Mrs. Miller herself had also been an early reader. She knew how to read in kindergarten, distinctly recalling that her grandmother had taught her to read. However, a high intelligence score does not make one an early reader. It has been established that children with a low IQ score can also become early readers. So there must be another explanation for Carrie's early reading development.

It is clear that the Millers highly valued reading, as did the nanny and the maternal grandmother. And they did not hesitate to encourage Carrie's reading development from an early age, and enjoyed stimulating it. They were also remarkably sensitive, and they gently and playfully based their reading interactions with the child on her interests and level of ability rather than on a prescribed instructional methodology. Carrie enjoyed all this attention, and was open to learn.

Sesame Street

But "things really started to happen between two and three," Mrs. Miller recalled. Jenny had just been born, and the "father took over" most of the reading activities with Carrie. He held long elaborate conversations with her, patiently responding to her countless questions. And he read to her for "hours a day." The nanny also decided it was time to start preparing Carrie for writing, and she began playing with her a variety of games around the shapes of letters. She used matchsticks to form the letter shapes, recalling a similar activity in her own daughter's kindergarten experience years ago.

Furthermore, Mrs. Baker urged the Millers to buy a television set so that Carrie could start watching *Sesame Street* and benefit from that program. (They were so immersed in their work that they had never bothered to buy a television.) And so, at the urging of Mrs. Baker the Millers did buy a set. And from age two until she was three and started going to nursery school, Carrie watched *Sesame Street* every morning and sometimes also in the afternoon. Once she started attending an all-day preschool, she watched television on the average of no more than half an hour a day. "She now looks at it while doing other things," Mrs. Miller commented.

Sound Games

In response to Carrie's growing interest in the sounds of letters, the parents also started playing sounds games with Carrie. For example, beginning with the letter *C*, for Carrie, mom or dad would call out, "Let's play the sound game, Carrie, C-C-C-C-C-C . . . what other words begin with the C-C-C-C sound?" And Carrie would come up with several words that begin with the *C* sound. Playing this game, they would go through the alphabet, and she loved it, Mrs. Miller recalled. It was also a good car game, she explained. "We tried to use every moment for learning." "What word begins with an *A*? A-A-A," the mother would call out to Carrie while driving. "What word begins with a *B*? B-B-B," she would continue, and through the alphabet they would go, with Carrie responding to each challenge.

For Christmas, when she was two and a half, the Millers gave Carrie a set of magnetic letters, in uppercase and lowercase. She liked to play with the letters on the refrigerator, enjoying at first to do matching activities—matching the letters of the same color; matching the letters of a kind, the *R*s, the *B*s, the *C*s; and then matching the numbers. One day, her mother started casually forming simple words with those letters on the refrigerator door: *Mom*, *Dad*, *Baby*. Mrs. Baker soon followed up writing words on slips of paper for Carrie to read. When Mrs. Miller would come home from work, she would find lists of words all over the house, she recalled.

Sometimes the nanny would form words with the letter blocks, and Carrie would try to make the same words with additional letters, silently reading the words. Or Mrs. Baker would playfully engage Carrie in spontaneous word games and Carrie would continue to work/play with the same words in the evening with her mother. Sometimes she would copy words from a book, arranging them with her plastic letters, then carefully comparing her words with the printed words in the book, Mrs. Miller recalled. "Is it the same?" she would ask? "Is it the same?" This was a daily routine for quite some time, with Carrie focusing on each new group of words for a period of about two weeks. And then, following a period of several months playing these word games, Carrie slowly began to read by herself from familiar books. She started with *Best Mother Goose Ever*, her first and favorite book of nursery rhymes, enjoying showing off her ability to her parents and nanny, Mrs. Miller recalled.

An Experience with Nursery School

And what about nursery school? Was her reading development affected perhaps by a sensitive teacher who may have given her some individualized attention at the right moments? As we shall see, not only did she *not* learn to read in nursery school, but Carrie's development was actually slowed down because of an insensitive teacher. The summer she turned three, Carrie started going to nursery school. The program her parents selected had a good reputation and she was exposed there to Hap Palmer's music. She was particularly fond of his song about the letters, one of Palmer's best, Mrs. Miller recounted. Carrie liked that song so much that her parents, who were unable to find it in a local record store, borrowed it from the nursery school to make a copy for home. She loved to dramatize that song. And the Millers cut out large letters from construction paper for her play, and she would walk/dance the letters around the living room and around the dining room table, listening to the music and lyrics. "It reinforced her letter knowledge," Mrs. Miller recalled. That summer was very pleasant, and Carrie was happy, her mother reflected.

But then, in the fall, when she was three years, two months old, a setback occurred in Carrie's reading activities. Her nursery school got new teachers. Their program was basically play-oriented with a focus on the socioemotional development of children. At first the Millers were pleased, believing Carrie was doing well. And when a teacher started to report that Carrie was timid and withdrawn, they were not too concerned, knowing she had always been like that. But then Carrie began to feel stifled. By spring "they took books away from her," and "she began to feel pressured to socialize," Mrs. Miller recounted. Moreover, "she was given to feel that reading was not a desirable activity." Carrie was becoming increasingly unhappy in that program. Often she did not want to go to school, "Because I am different," she'd explain to her parents. The mother began to worry that early reading may become a source of problems for Carrie, and she stopped working with her, more or less, she explained. Traumatized by the teacher's negative remarks, the parents even stopped buying books for Carrie. There was a period in which they just "floundered around reading library books," checking out primarily the "classics"—*Cinderella, Snow White,* and *Peter Pan.* To compensate, Carrie played a lot with Play Dough, making the letters of the alphabet and enjoying the soothing effect of the soft material, Mrs. Miller recalled.

In my conversation with Mrs. C., Carrie's teacher, a year after she attended her program, I could still sense the deep animosity that existed between her and Carrie's parents. "Carrie was the most timid and fearful child that I had ever seen," Mrs. C. said. She considered the Millers to be pushy parents with excessively high mental expectation of their child. She did not think that Carrie knew how to read the year she was in her group, implying that the parents were only bragging about her ability. "She probably learned to read in her present school," she added.

Toward the end of that miserable year in nursery school, the Millers decided to move Carrie to another school, "the only school in town that offered individualized attention for early readers," they explained. And when Carrie went to the new place for an interview, she reportedly read the signs in the hallways. "She can read!" Dr. Miller recalled the remarks of the staff person who walked with them. Two of Carrie's teachers at the new school confirmed the parents' account about her reading ability. "She was reading well at the beginning of the school year, for a child of her age," one of them told me. They worked on her socialization skills, and "they took reading and made her feel that this is a good achievement . . . that she can share her knowledge with other children," Mrs. Miller recounted. The parents are very pleased with the new program.

PROUD TO READ

Once again Carrie was proud of her reading ability. And when she demonstrated to her parents her ability to read a book all by herself, from beginning to end, the Millers got so excited they made a special long-distance call to Carrie's grandmother to have her listen to how well Carrie could read. She continued to be interested in the same fairy tales she had enjoyed the previous year, only now reading the more difficult versions. One of her favorite books at four years, ten months was *The Big Golden Book of Fairy Tales* by Lornie Leete-Hodge. She has also started to read books about dinosaurs, fossils, and skeletons. She often reads them in silence, asking her parents for help with difficult words. Still, despite her increasingly independent reading ability, Carrie continues to enjoy listening to her parents' daily readings to her.

SOLVING THE PUZZLE

We see that although they had never intended to teach Carrie to read, maintaining that one cannot "teach" reading to a preschooler, the Millers were far from being passive bystanders in this regard. While they viewed early reading ability to be innate, an ability that a child either has or does not, the anecdotes they related reveal a rich repertoire of reading and writing interactions between them and Carrie from an early age. The role of the nanny should not be overlooked either. Having no other responsibilities but the care of the girls, she, too, spent substantial time every day entertaining and stimulating Carrie with reading- and writing-related activities, among others.

These three adults sensitively followed Carrie's interests, curiosity, and level of ability, and based their literacy interactions with her on these. Once she showed an interest, they would respond with a spontaneous relevant game or activity. Or, sensing a budding ability, they would playfully challenge and stimulate it. They read to her a lot while pointing at the words; they encouraged her to acquire a sight vocabulary; they taught her the names, the shapes, and the sounds of the letters; they helped her with spelling and forming words—all playfully and intuitively done—using many games that came to mind, or were recalled from their own childhood, picked up from other resources, or creatively invented by them. Moreover, whenever Carrie demonstrated some ability, they got excited and showed their excitement to her. They were truly happy, accepting any ability as proof that she was developing well, and that they were not such bad parents after all, even if leaving her with a nanny. "It is very nice when you have your first child, and are a working mother with all those guilt feelings, to find that your child is not going to be retarded," Mrs. Miller explained. It is important to emphasize that the goal throughout these parental interactions with Carrie was her mental stimulation and development, and having a good time together, rather than teaching her to read. The child's eventual mastery of reading was almost a by-product of these adults' desire to stimulate her and have a good time with her.

It is interesting to observe that while no one had planned to teach Carrie to read and no one had followed any systematic method of reading instruction with her, Carrie did experience, very much like Sean, a natural course of development that followed a distinct order. A careful analysis of Carrie's chronology of reading behavior reveals an emerging learning process that was based on a number of distinct stages or phases of development. Again, these stages were very similar to the stages experienced by Sean.

THE STAGES IN CARRIE'S READING DEVELOPMENT

First, there was a period in which Carrie gained general awareness of books and print, which started almost from day one. This period included the parents' daily readings, her scanning of geometric patterns, her interest in print, rocking to the rhythm of nursery rhymes, playing with letter blocks, and so on. The parents' reading to Carrie, throughout this period, was an emotionally loaded activity, a lifeline between them and their child, with a soothing effect for both parties.

Once she was twelve months old, a change occurred in Carrie's reading behavior. Her interest began to be more focused, and she began to acquire a sight vocabulary. Soon she developed an interest in letters. For a period of several months she would now show simultaneous interest in learning the letters and recognizing isolated words.

At twenty-five months, another change occurred. Carrie grew increasingly receptive to the sounds of the letters, perceiving that each letter has a distinct sound, in addition to a name. And about half a year later, around thirty months, she became interested in the makeup of words, realizing one day that words are actually formed with letters. For the following several months, she would attempt again and again to form words with her magnetic letters or the letter blocks, mastering the concept.

Once she internalized the way words are formed, beginning at thirty months, she started to read from easy, familiar picture books. By thirty-six months, she could read by herself an unfamiliar picture book. By fifty-eight months, she was reading books on dinosaurs and fossils, enjoying the content as well as the illustrations.

Although reading- and writing-related activities emerged spontaneously in the Miller home and apparently unsystematically, the stages of development that evolved had an intrinsic order that can be summarized as follows:

Stage 1: Carrie gained an awareness of books and print (starting from day one).

Stage 2: Carrie acquired a sight vocabulary in parallel to letter knowledge (from about twelve months).

Stage 3: Carrie learned the sounds of the letters (starting at twenty-five months).

Stage 4: Carrie formed words with magnetic letters and began to read easy, familiar picture books (starting at thirty months).

Stage 5: Carrie developed the ability to read unfamiliar picture books (thirty-six months).

Stage 6: Carrie read for enjoyment of content (ongoing at fifty-eight months).

Just as in Sean's case, each of these stages was characterized by a distinct reading concept involving a particular skill (such as knowing the names of the letters, understanding that each letter has a sound, or that words are formed with these sounds, etc.). Each concept and its corresponding skill became of central interest to Carrie, while she was in that stage. She would focus on that skill and play/practice it extensively for a period of several months until it was mastered. And then she would move on to the next stage, characterized by a new concept and skill that needed to be internalized before she could become a reader. While focusing on learning the new skill, she would continue to use the skills she had mastered in the previous stages, but she would no longer need to spend much time or effort to learn these.

Chapter Five

Two-Year-Old Brian

Young children begin to learn about reading and writing initially in their homes and communities as they observe and participate in culturally situated literacy practices.

> —Victoria Purcell-Gates, "Stories, Coupons,
> and the TV Guide: Relationships
> between Home Literacy Experiences
> and Emergent Literacy Knowledge"

THE GIOVANNI FAMILY

Identified as a reader when he was only two years, six months old, Brian is the youngest reader portrayed in this book. Like Sean and Carrie, he learned to read in a nonsystematic, informal manner. His parents maintain that they never intended to teach Brian, and that his achievement is the result of his own initiative. They helped and guided him, they say, but were "more or less on the fence," neither wanting to push the child nor discourage him.

The Giovanni family—Alex, Barb, Brian, and ten-month-old Michelle—lives in a tiny, turn-of-the-century house located at the edge of the city limits. Both parents grew up in that neighborhood and maternal as well as paternal grandparents still reside there today. Also uncles and aunts from both sides of the family live in the area, and members of this extended family get together often. They are rooted, and they dote on their youngest generation: Brian, Michelle, and a three-year-old cousin. Barb and Alex are in their mid-twenties, outgoing, articulate, and relaxed. Each has an associate's degree. Alex is a glass worker at a local company; Barb is a full-time homemaker. She plans to get a part-time job once the children are in school. Children and family appear to be the focus of the Giovannis' life.

Their home is cozy, bright, and neatly kept. Brian's room has a Mickey Mouse decor—bedspread, curtains, clothes hanger, three statues, a doll, and a hooked-rug on the wall. A cross-stitch prayer on another wall, which Brian knows by heart, and a few favorite books are the only print-related things in this room. The children's large assortment of toys and books is kept downstairs in a closet by the living room. The small living room and dining room area forms the cozy hub of their waking-hours activities.

ANOTHER NATURAL READER

The first question that comes to mind is about similarities between Brian, Sean, and Carrie's reading development. Is there any common thread in their personality or home background that could explain their natural early reading development? Friendly, outgoing, with smooth brown hair, large blue eyes, and, to use his father words, a face that "always smiles," Brian is energetic, excitable, and determined. He is an "extremely happy" child, both parents concurred, and is easy to handle. He is also curious and sometimes stubborn. And when he throws a temper tantrum, which he occasionally likes to do, the parents say that they just leave him alone to cool off.

At thirty-four months, Brian's articulation is not yet completely clear. He pronounces the *L* sound, for instance, as a *W*. And although Barb is a stay-at-home mom who enjoys having Brian around, the parents started kicking around the idea of sending him to nursery school, in part to improve his articulation. But they have a hard time deciding which type of program would really benefit him. "He still does not know how to play with children," Barb reflects, "he either runs around or just hugs and kisses." And so, at the time of the study, Brian's peer inter-action was limited to some shared time (not necessarily shared play) with a neighbor boy of the same age, and an occasional play date with his cousin who is five months older. He likes to play with Michelle, his sister, Barb notes, having recently started reading stories to her, promoting his as well as her development.

A diagnosed asthmatic condition does not seem to worry the Giovannis too much. Alex used to have similar allergies when he was a child and eventually grew out of them. The par-ents seem confident that Brian will outgrow the condition as well. In the meantime, since he is allergic to wheat, rye, choco-late, peanuts, dust, and possibly some other allergens, Brian is kept on monthly allergy shots.

It is difficult to draw a simple comparison between Brian and the other two children's personalities and family back-grounds, each being so different. And yet the fact remains that all three managed to learn to read early, in a nonsystematic manner. What could have induced little Brian's early reading de-velopment, in that simple and unassuming home environment? "He has an excellent memory, and a keen perception for details," Barb and Alex tried to explain, "and such a long attention span that he can maintain interest on a task for over an hour." The parents believe that these qualities contributed to Brian's early reading ability. "He is not too good with his imagination," Barb added, and he does not play "pretend games" like other children. "He is only interested in tangible facts such as written words."

He is also "a great TV watcher," Mrs. Giovanni added. Brian started to watch television "since he could see." From early on he was attracted to commercials, and whenever a commercial would appear on the screen, he would stop what-ever he was doing to watch it. Barb thinks that repetitive com-mercials stimulated Brian's reading development. Now he watches three to four hours a day of children's programs such as *Sesame Street*, *Mr. Rogers' Neighborhood*, and *Romper Room*, programs that highlight letter knowledge and word recogni-tion, and these have added to Brian's reading knowledge, Barb says. (He also watches an unspecified daily amount of adult television whenever he is in the room while his parents are viewing. "But he does not really watch those," his mother remarked somewhat uncomfortably.)

Yet, many children watch *Sesame Street* and other television programs every day, and they do not become early readers. It is therefore unlikely that television was the dominant factor in Brian's reading development. So what was the impetus for his early development?

When he does not watch television, Brian likes to keep busy with a variety of reading related activities, and these can entertain him for several hours a day, Mrs. Giovanni declared. Included among these, for example, is an assortment of reading games that he plays with his mother, or reading books with one parent or the other, reading by himself, working in one of his workbooks, or playing with his alphabet letters.

Like all children, Brian also enjoys nonreading-related activities. Among his favorites are block building and doing puzzles. At thirty-three months, for example, he had the ability to put together a twenty-four-piece puzzle without a frame. Both parents believe that his work with puzzles contributed to Brian's early reading ability—sharpening his visual perception and memory, and improving his eye/hand coordination. (It is interesting that drawing, with its possible effect on reading/writing development, did not appeal to Brian, and he has only recently started to scribble). He loves music. He likes to sing and listen to MTV and records. Light rock is his favorite, according to his mother, in particular songs by Barbara Streisand and Diana Ross, the type of music his parents enjoy. "He was always fond of music," Barb reflected, and from early on he was put to bed with background music to calm and relax him.

Why was Brian so interested in those reading-related activities? Could an exceptionally high level of intelligence explain his early reading interest? As it turned out, it was not possible to assess his intelligence level at the time of the study. He was too young for a formal assessment. And all of our attempts, when Brian was two years, ten months, to obtain a standard score on the Peabody Picture Vocabulary Test failed to reach a ceiling. The administration of the Stanford Binet Intelligence Scale was also unsuccessful. In both cases, the tester concluded that the tests were invalid because of Brian's young age and his inability to sit still for the duration of the formal testing session. So, what could explain his early reading ability? Before we attempt to delve deeper into that puzzle, let us first find out how well Brian could actually read.

HOW WELL COULD BRIAN READ?

Brian's parents did not realize at first that their son's reading development was advanced in any manner, and it took the grandparents to actually make them aware of it, they say. At the age of thirty months, he was formally identified as a reader at the Early Childhood Research Center of the University at Buffalo. And once the Giovannis volunteered to participate in my study, I went to their home to make a more comprehensive assessment of Brian's ability. He was thirty-three months old then and I thought that the informal home environment would be more suitable for a testing situation for a child of that age.

We were sitting on the living room couch and Brian appeared comfortable and eager to show off his ability. I started with a challenge, telling him I had heard that he could read. "Is it true?" I asked him. "Can you really read? Would you like to show me?" He was eager to show off his ability and read fluently the six criterion sentences. I proceeded with an informal selection from several picture books. To my surprise, and unlike the older children in the study, it was interesting to see how easy it was to move Brian from one book to another. He was totally absorbed in the mechanics of reading, and in demonstrating his ability, and did not seem to care much for the content of the stories.

He read fluently, with no errors, the title and nine sentences (three pages) from *Cowboy Sam and Dandy* by Edna W. Chandler, a preprimer-level book. He then read the title and nine sentences in *What Do They Do?* by Carla Greene, a primer-level book. He read these sentences quickly and fluently, making only one repeated error: whenever the text said *badge* he read it as *bandage* (bandage is probably a more meaningful word than badge for a boy who is not yet three years old).

I stepped up the difficulty of the text and asked Brian to read from *Sailor Jack and Bluebell's Dive* by Selma and Jack Wassermann, a First Reader. He read the title and seven sentences fluently, making no mistakes. Then, reading eight sentences from *Titch* by Pat Hutchins, a Second Reader, he made only one error, saying *bicycle* instead of *tricycle*. Having no other graded picture books with me, I had to stop the assessment at that level, concluding that at the age of two years, nine months, Brian had the technical ability to read from any picture book. Although I made no formal attempt to assess his comprehension level, answers he gave to several content-related questions indicated a general understanding of the text on that level.

Two weeks later, when Brian came to the campus for his Peabody and Stanford Binet tests, he did not read as well. The unfamiliar environment of the campus playroom was too exciting, making it difficult for him to concentrate on the reading task. And when I showed him a picture book and asked him to read from it, his attention was drawn to other objects in the room. When he finally agreed to read, he was fluent only for a few sentences, and then, encountering an unfamiliar word, he stopped, refusing to even give it a try. Later on, to my surprise, when I casually asked him to read words off cans and food containers stacked on a shelf, his reading was remarkable. He did not make a single mistake, not even with difficult words. "He could probably read 99 percent of any word list I would write for him," Barb remarked. This apparent discrepancy in his ability to read isolated words compared with the words in a text may indicate he was using different mental strategies in reading these two types of text. The discrepancy between his performance at home compared to that at the campus only proves the importance of a relaxed environment for the assessment of young children.

HOW DID HE DO IT?

So how did Brian do it? How did he acquire this level of reading proficiency at such a young age? On first impression there appears to be nothing unusual in Brian's home environment, or personality makeup, that could explain this early development. Yes, he did have a good concentration ability, keen visual perception, and memory, but so have many other children of similar age and background. Apart for his asthmatic condition, and the resulting lack of interest in physical activity, his daily life was not that different from other children of similar age with an intact family and a stay-at-home mom. Except, perhaps, for the somewhat greater role of reading-related games in his home. The Giovannis did mention they had engaged in many letter-sound and word games with Brian. Is there a clue here? Let us take a closer look at some of their anecdotes regarding Brian's reading development.

As they recount, at the age of eight months, Brian had two books, one made of cloth and one made of plastic. But his primary interest at the time was not in the stories or the pictures, and not in the printed words in these books, but in their pages. These pages fascinated him and he wanted continuously to turn them, Barb recalls, apparently enjoying his growing facility to manipulate them. Nothing else was noteworthy about his reading behavior at that time, says Barb.

At eighteen months, Brian showed some interest in magazines. Barb and Alex had subscriptions to *Parents'*, *Good Housekeeping*, and *Hot Rod*, and Brian would often flip through these magazines, sometimes focusing his attention on the advertisements. Between eighteen and nineteen months, he would often fix his gaze on words and letters in the advertisements. He also started to pay some attention to the newspaper. Whenever his parents would read a magazine, Brian would come and snuggle by them trying to get their attention, and repeatedly asking what they were reading. Slowly, they began to point to simple words—*baby*, *powder*, *car*—words they thought would attract his interest. And they read those words to him. They believed this was a typical activity between toddlers and parents, driven by a child's endless curiosity and desire for attention.

A Traumatic Experience

A hospitalization event, when Brian was nineteen months old, really symbolizes for the Giovannis the beginning of his accelerated reading development. And this event stands out as a landmark in their memory. It was a simple case of bronchitis, they say, but because of his asthmatic condition, which restricted his oral medication intake, Brian had to receive the medication intravenously. And so he was hospitalized for three days. The experience was traumatic for the child and his parents, and the events that followed are vividly etched in Barb and Alex's memory.

Brian was discharged from the hospital with the specific instruction to be kept physically calm and relaxed. The Giovannis had no choice but to spend substantial amounts of time with him, entertaining and keeping him busy. Trying their best to follow the pediatrician's advice, it dawned on them that reading-related activities could be ideal for their situation; they are quiet, simple, entertaining, and even educational. And it was during that posthospitalization period, when they were closely supervising Brian, that they began to "notice things," Barb recounted.

First, they noticed that Brian was recognizing television ads. He could recognize names of local supermarkets and department stores, as well as brand names of household products. Then, they observed that he was also recognizing advertising words in newspapers and magazines. Moreover, whenever they would take him to a shopping mall, Brian would point at store signs and read their names. "He probably recognized them from television or the newspaper," his parents explained. During this same period, Brian started to match his alphabet letters with the letters in the newspaper. They were "dumbfounded" by his incredible memory, both parents remarked.

The Effect of a Good Television Program

At twenty months a new dimension was added to Brian's reading behavior, when he began to "really" watch *Sesame Street*. Soon he was watching the program daily, often two or three times. He enjoyed the fast-moving pace, Barb recalled. She would often view the program with him, trying to learn about adults' interaction with children, an aspect that is prominently featured in *Sesame Street*. "*Sesame Street* helped Brian learn the alphabet," said Barb.

Soon after that, once they noticed Brian's growing interest in letters, the Giovannis bought him a workbook: *Thinking, Reading, and Doing*. It was a Golden Book for the preschool level and they thought it would give him something interesting to do, and keep him busy for a while. Brian would chat endlessly about the letters and the signs in that workbook, recalled his parents. "He was interested in workbooks even before he showed interest in books," Barb said.

Other family members soon began to notice Brian's growing interest in print, and an uncle gave him a set of alphabet blocks. Then his grandmother gave him a Winnie-the-Pooh nesting-block set. (That set consisted of colorful cardboard blocks that could be either nested in a 7 × 7-inch-square base block or stacked one on top of the other in gradually diminishing size to form a three-foot tower. Between one and four letters were printed on each block, and as the tower was erected, the letters could be arranged from bottom to top in alphabetical order. Numbers appeared on another side of each block; sections making up a tall tree were printed on the third side; and pictures illustrating the story of Winnie-the-Pooh were printed on the fourth side.) This nesting-block set turned out to be of special importance in Brian's reading development. He would play with it again and again, and "it was very helpful for learning the alphabet," Barb and Alex recalled. Within a month of playing/working with that set, and watching *Sesame Street* daily, Brian mastered the alphabet.

Letter Games

What was Barb and Alex's role throughout that period? Were they actively engaged in the ongoing learning process? They began to play a variety of letter games with Brian. For instance, they would point to a letter, name it, and have Brian repeat its name. Or, in another game, the mother would challenge the boy, playfully saying, "Show me an *A*," "Show me a *B*," "Show me a *C*," and going through the alphabet, Brian would point to the correct letter. While the purpose of these games—which were intuitively invented or adapted from one source or another—was first and foremost to entertain Brian, they also stimulated, encouraged, and further developed his interest, and thus facilitated his learning. The Giovannis recalled that within a matter of weeks he was able to recognize the letters, name them, and recite them in alphabetical order. By twenty-one months, he could also recognize his name whenever one of his parents would print it. Happy to observe his rapid development, the parents decided to give Brian another workbook—*Sizes, Shapes and Numbers*—to help him learn the numbers from one to ten. "But numbers did not excite him as much as the letters," Barb and Alex recalled.

Pointing Out Words

Once he was able to recite the alphabet from memory, Brian no longer needed the letters to be in front of him, said

Barb. And they were excited to see him, at twenty-three months, beginning to point out direction words in stores: *exit*, *in*, *out*. He also learned to recognize road sign words such as *Stop*, from one of his coloring books. "This says *Stop*," Barb would tell him, pointing at that word. And he would remember.

Brian's reputation as an early reader was growing, and for his second birthday, an uncle gave him a chalkboard. Barb then started to print words on that board—*Mom*, *Dad*, *Michelle*, *Grandma*, *Papa*, *yes*, *no*, *dog*, *cat*—simple words, reflecting his daily life, that she thought would capture his interest. It was a spontaneous idea, she said, intended primarily to entertain Brian and mentally stimulate him, more than teach him to read. Why not? she thought, and he caught on to it. She would write a word, read it to him, and have Brian repeat the word after her. And, after one round, he would retain the word and was able to recognize it whenever he would see that word again. He did not care much for books at the time, both parents related, only for words. And when they tried to interest him in a picture book titled *People in the Family* (which was a Sesame Street publication aimed at his age level), he showed no interest. Only words related to his daily life would attract Brian's attention at the time.

And so we can see how the Giovannis kept stimulating the boy, making reading activities playful and entertaining both for Brian and for themselves. The primary objective of these activities, it is important to emphasize, was the mental stimulation of the child and his entertainment—while keeping him quietly busy—rather than teaching him to read. The fine degree of sensitivity in their interaction, sensitivity to their child's interests and sensitivity to the level of his ability, is noteworthy. These parents truly understood their child's needs and were in tune with him. And he was eager to respond to their playful challenges. Without this fine degree of sensitivity, Brian's reading development probably would not have progressed as much as it did at that early age.

What happened next? At twenty-five months, Brian had a sight vocabulary of some thirty words, Barb recounted. He also started to arrange his block letters in alphabetical order. So Barb decided to start playing a new letter game with him: "What begins with an *A*?" she would ask, and Brian would reply with a word beginning with the letter *A*. "What begins with a *B*?" she would continue, "with a *C*?" and so they'd go through the alphabet, with Brian shouting a word for each letter the mother was calling. They always went through all the letters in alphabetical order, Barb remarked. "He just loved it."

Putting Words Together

About two months after receiving the chalkboard, the Giovannis decided to buy Brian a set of magnetic letters that could be used on the backside of the chalkboard. "The chalks were too messy for him," Barb explained, "and he didn't like the feel of the powder on his fingers." He enjoyed lining up the magnetic letters on the board in alphabetical order, and soon started to spell simple words with these letters. The parents vividly recall that *sport* was the first word he could spell, copying it from a newspaper his father was reading. Soon he would spell from memory simple words such as *dog*, *car*, or *cat*, Barb said. Interestingly, Brian first preferred to spell with the block letters more than with the magnetic letters. The sheer number of the latter was too confusing for him, Barb thinks. She may have also contributed to this, she admitted, preferring to take out the block letters more often then the magnetic letters to play with in the backyard. "It was easier to pick them up," she confided. In any case, by twenty-seven months, Brian's sight vocabulary grew to some fifty words.

A Fascination with Puzzles

There was another factor, according to the Giovannis, that may have contributed to Brian's early reading development: an apparent fascination with puzzles. At twenty-seven months his interest in puzzles was so strong, Barb recounted, it was almost as strong as his interest in reading. "It's a toss-up between books and puzzles," she said. The Giovannis believe that Brian's fascination and preoccupation with his puzzles had sharpened his visual perception and memory, and improved his eye/hand coordination. There can be little doubt about Brian's interest in fine motor activities.

An Interest in Dictionaries

At age two, Brian's life appeared almost idyllic. He had a secure, supportive home environment. He was surrounded by a doting extended family rooted in the community. His parents were energetic and eager to facilitate his development. And he absorbed a lot from that nourishing environment. Slowly, Brian's interest in his mother's lists of words grew into an interest in dictionaries. At twenty-seven months, his parents bought him the *Rainbow Dictionary*, a Wright Collins World publication, and at twenty-eight months, they gave him *Reading Fun*, a coloring dictionary by Golden Press. Soon thereafter, they gave him the *Picture Dictionary* by Playmore. He loved to go over the words in those dictionaries, Barb said. She would read to him a few words and he would memorize them. He was still not interested in stories, only in words. And whenever one of his parents would try to read to him a story, he would divert the attention to words; "What's that?" he would ask, pointing at one word or another. Or, turning the page over, he would try to see what words appeared on the following page. Wisely, the Giovannis did not pressure him and went along with that, sensitively adjusting their reading interactions to his interest and ability level.

Writing Short Messages

And then, from writing lists of words, Barb switched to writing simple sentences on Brian's blackboard. "I love you," she would write, or "Brian is a good boy," "Michelle is a girl," and so on. She thought he was ready for that, and that he would enjoy these messages. She also wondered if these simple sentences would help him understand that "words together mean something." He was about twenty-nine months old at the time. And after awhile, Brian slowly started to read sentences from his books. Furthermore, he began to pay attention to the content of the stories.

The First Books

Obviously, the next step was to buy a number of picture books to satisfy Brian's new growing interest in stories. Included among the first books his parents bought were *Mickey and Friends*, a Disney publication; *The Fox Finds a Friend*, another Disney publication; and *The Country Puppy*, published by Dutton-Elsevire. These books had to be read to Brian over and over again. *People in the Family*, the Sesame Street publication that was one of the old books in the house, and the first the Giovannis could read to Brian from beginning to end, became a favorite. For about two weeks, Alex had to read that book to Brian every night before putting him to bed. Pointing at each word while reading, and making Brian repeat after him "word by word, then sentence by sentence," the boy soon memorized the story and was also able to recognize individual words when pointed at out of context.

And so began a new phase of literacy development. Once Brian could "read" *People in the Family*, Alex started to read with him other books, making sure the boy repeated every story after him word by word, sentence by sentence. While the first book took two weeks to learn, following books took only three or four evenings each. Many words were repeated in the stories, Alex explained, making it easier for Brian to recognize them. Whenever Brian would come across a difficult word, Alex would read that word and ask Brian to repeat it.

Barb would play spontaneous word-and-sound games during the day as she was doing her chores around the house, and Alex would work with Brian in the evenings—reading to him, and making him read after him word by word, sentence by sentence. This routine went on for about four months, Barb related, until shortly before Christmas, when Brian was thirty-two months old. By thirty months, Barb also started to read books with him. But "he really started to read" by thirty-two months, Alex explained. Up until then he never sounded out words, he said, not even the difficult ones, instead reading by visual memory alone. Whenever he would come across a difficult word, he would ask one of his parents for help. But at thirty-two months, once he started to read books by himself, Brian started to sound out the words he could not recognize by sight.

Realizing that he needed some help with the sounds of the letters, the Giovannis started a new game: the rhyme game. "What rhymes with *mommy*?" Barb would ask, and one of Brian's favorite responses would be *salami*. "What rhymes with *teacher*?" the mother would continue, and Brian would often respond with *meecher*. His responses could be with real words or with nonsensical fun words, both were accepted. And then, on Christmas morning, when he opened one of his gifts, the book of *The Three Bears*, the Giovannis realized to their amazement that he could really read that book. He had never seen that book before, Barb remarked, nor had he heard the story, and yet, he could read it right away from cover to cover, sounding out each difficult word. Moreover, a few days later, when he was at his grandmother's house and Brian found there Dr. Seuss's popular book *Green Eggs and Ham*, he could also read that book all by himself. "It was then that he started to read books to his sister," Barb remarked.

Brian's comprehension ability slowly caught up with his technical reading skill, and at age thirty-four months, "Brian also gets the content of the story," his father related. He can now comprehend whatever he is reading while doing the actual reading, whereas before, "he was not interested in the meaning while reading, but was more interested in saying the words." Brian's grandmother gave him a new workbook about spelling, to help him polish his knowledge of the letters' sounds. And Barb started a new game she named the "cheering game." "Give me an *M*," she would say, and Brian would say "*M*," "Give me an *O*," she would continue, and Brian would say "*O*." "Give me an *M*," she would say again, and Brian would say "*M*." "What does it spell?" she would ask, and Brian would quickly reply, "*Mom*." And so they'd go through spelling several words until both would tire of that activity.

SOLVING THE MYSTERY

Let us ask once again, How did Brian learn to read? While his parents maintain that they never intended to teach him and that his achievement is the result of his own initiative, their anecdotes reveal that they did spend substantial amounts of time with Brian on reading-related activities. What was the driving force behind these interactions? What kept alive the interest of this child of two and a half in these activities when so many children his age show no interest? Was it his genes, his superb visual perception and memory, the reading games his parents played with him, or perhaps some other environmental factor?

It seems to me that the driving force behind this continuous interest was the simple stimulation of a preschooler's curious mind along with good parental attitudes. Included among these were the Giovannis' enthusiasm about early reading, an uncorrupted instinctive belief in their child's ability to comprehend simple print-related concepts, and an intuitive faith in their ability to support their son's development. All these were combined with a dose of continual encouragement; sensitivity to their son's level of ability; and a willingness to play, stimulate, and work with him on that level. There is no doubt in my mind that this combination of attitudes facilitated Brian's early reading development.

While activities occurred naturally, spontaneously, with little planning, often prompted by the child's queries, interest, or curiosity, the parents' instinctive desire to stimulate and facilitate Brian's development was very strong and actively engaged. Their appreciation for good reading ability, and understanding that early reading is desirable because it can give the child a head start in school and promote a feeling of self-confidence, was at the root of their motivation. Brian's asthmatic condition has also helped in this case, making quiet reading-related activities especially appealing.

While they say that they sat on the fence, and in all honesty believe that Brian mastered the different reading skills because of an innate ability, the data show a different picture, clearly revealing their active engagement in the child's reading development. Once they realized that he could retain what they were showing him, the ball started rolling. Instinctively, the Giovannis used many good didactic techniques in their reading interactions with Brian, and they sensitively chose activities that were often playful in nature. They had an intuitive understanding that young children learn best through play, and the literacy interactions in the Giovanni home were almost some kind of family game. This is why the Giovannis never considered themselves to be teaching Brian but rather playing and stimulating him.

Playfully, they taught him the names of the letters and some sight vocabulary. Playfully, they worked with him on spelling and rhyming. Playfully, they taught him to read words and then sentences. And then patiently they read books with him, pointing at the words and encouraging him to repeat after them word by word, sentence by sentence. Their intuitive sense of timing—when Brian was ready for each of these activities—is noteworthy and important, reducing the amount of frustration from both parents and child.

There is one final question in the puzzle of Brian's reading development, and this question has to do with the learning process. Was this process random or did some intrinsic order exist in its development? After all, none of the Giovannis had followed any manual of reading instruction, and neither the child nor his parents had any prior knowledge about reading development or its methodology. Have the various literacy-related activities occurred in some intrinsic natural order or was there nothing like that here?

Following a careful analysis of the data, it was amazing to realize that Brian, like Sean and Carrie, had experienced a gradual sequence of reading behavior that had a distinct pattern of development. This sequence included several steps or stages, each manifesting itself through a particular reading behavior, and this reading behavior indicated the acquisition of a new reading concept.

THE STAGES IN BRIAN'S READING DEVELOPMENT

First, there was a preliminary period in which Brian gained general awareness of books and print. Ongoing at eight months and lasting for several months, Brian showed interest in magazines, turning the pages of books, and television commercials. Once he had some general awareness of books and print, starting from the age of eighteen months, a dramatic change was observed. He started to show interest in the alphabet letters and he began to learn their names. Simultaneously, he started to acquire a beginning sight vocabulary.

By twenty-seven months, Brian started to put together simple words with his magnetic letters or letter blocks. This activity indicated that he had the conceptual understanding that words are composed of letters. And his attempts to form words with his letters were, in fact, a beginning form of writing. He had the desire to write, and the conceptual ability to form a word, but he did not yet have the fine finger dexterity and the eye/hand coordination necessary for writing with a pencil or any other conventional writing instrument. So he "wrote" words with his block or magnetic letters.

About two months later, around the age of twenty-nine months, another change occurred. Brian's interest in forming words switched to an interest in sentences and stories. And he began to voraciously read stories with his parents. While his letter knowledge continued to improve through the games he played with Barb, there was, at around thirty-one months, an emphasis on the sounds of the letters rather than their names and their order in the alphabet. At thirty-two months, Brian began to sound out unfamiliar words, and slowly, he started to read unfamiliar books by himself. At thirty-four months, he could read an unfamiliar picture book all by himself, with good comprehension ability. The steps in this sequence of development can be summarized as follows:

Stage 1: A preliminary period of gaining general awareness of books and print (ongoing at eight months).

Stage 2: Learning to identify the letters and acquire a sight vocabulary (starting from eighteen months).

Stage 3: Putting together words (starting at twenty-seven months).

Stage 4: Reading familiar books with parental help (starting at twenty-nine months).

Stage 5: Learning the sounds of letters (around thirty-one months).

Stage 6: Sounding out unfamiliar words (starting at thirty-two months).

Stage 7:   Reading unfamiliar picture books (at thirty-
four months).

This appears to be a remarkably logical and intrinsically ordered sequence of development. And as with Sean and Carrie,
each of the steps or stages in Brian's reading development was
apparently a prerequisite for the following stage, a necessary
rung in his ladder of reading development. The fact that three
children from three different environmental backgrounds had
experienced such a remarkably similar developmental process is
significant. The implications of that will be further discussed in
Chapter 9.

Chapter Six

————

Alicia's Story

But their manner of writing is very peculiar, being neither from the left to the right, like the Europeans; nor
from the right to the left, like the Arabians; nor from up
to down, like the Chinese; nor from down to up, like
the Cascagians, but aslant from one corner of the paper
to the other, like ladies in England.
                    —Jonathan Swift, *A Voyage to Lilliput*

THE GIBSON FAMILY

Alicia, the child of two music teachers, was identified as an early
reader when she was two years, eleven months old. Her mother
resigned from a twelve-year-long teaching career to be home
with her newborn baby. Once Mrs. Gibson noticed the girl's
growing interest in print, she was thrilled and filled with joy. It
had been worthwhile! she thought. My decision to be a full-time
mother will make a difference, and Alicia will be a brighter
child! Let us meet Alicia and her parents, and observe how two
professional teachers facilitated the natural reading development of their little girl.

The family includes the father, thirty-seven, the mother,
thirty-seven, and Alicia, at the time an only child, almost three

years old. The parents are natives of the region, and paternal grandparents as well as uncles and aunts live in the area. Family members often get together to celebrate birthdays and holidays. Both parents have a degree in music education: the father is a music teacher in a middle school; the mother was a music teacher in an elementary school. The paternal grandfather, now retired, was head of music instruction for the city's school system.

The Gibson home, located in a quiet suburban neighborhood, is neat and comfortably furnished. Stepping in, one is struck by the colorful profusion of African violets of all colors and shades, grown in specially designed lighted cases, covering the walls of the living room and dining room areas. Mrs. Gibson, who used to grow these flowers commercially, now grows them as a hobby.

As beautiful and colorful and time-consuming as these flowers are, "Alicia is the central focus of the family," her father declared during my visit to their home. Since leaving her teaching job, Mrs. Gibson has worked only sporadically as a substitute teacher. And she is the first to admit she missed her teaching job at first. But she is now content with her parenting role, she says, particularly since Alicia has started showing an interest in print. "Alicia needs me right now," Mrs. Gibson explained. And she devotes a great deal of time to the child, doing her best to facilitate her overall development, including reading. She is confident that had she worked outside the home, Alicia's reading development would not have come about as early as it did. And she is very happy about that early development.

Both parents are proud of Alicia's early reading ability, comparing it with the reading development of a twelve-year-old cousin, who reportedly could read the *National Geographic* by the time he was four years old. "It is important that they [preschool children] have something constructive to do and not just sit and vegetate for five or six years," Mrs. Gibson explained. "This is the time in which they develop the most. It's a shame if they just sit and do nothing," she said. "Alicia's early reading will give her an advantage when she goes to school," Mr. Gibson elaborated. "She will have one less thing to struggle with."

Acknowledging their active support of Alicia's reading development, it appears the Gibsons' only concern has been that they may be doing something wrong, and perhaps miss some important step in the process. They worry that this may come to haunt her later. They still hope to find some systematic approach for their work with Alicia. This will give them the reassurance that they are moving in the right direction, they say. In the meantime, they have been facilitating her development intuitively, stimulating and encouraging it in any way that makes sense to them.

Because of the unsystematic nature of the Gibsons' print interactions with Alicia, one can say that she learned to read naturally. Her reading development was stimulated much like her oral language development had been the year before. There is little understanding in our culture of that kind of reading development and little insight into the developmental process involved. For a long time the phenomenon has been attributed to some special (unknown) innate abilities of these children. But as discussed in Chapter 2, this perception is now changing. Alicia's story, like the other stories in this book, is among the few comprehensive accounts illustrating the process of natural reading development. It is therefore illuminating. Let us take a closer look at Alicia and her home environment, and the type of literacy interactions she experienced.

PORTRAIT OF ANOTHER NATURAL READER

Tall, with short blond hair and a mischievous twinkle in her eyes, Alicia was a big baby at birth and was three weeks overdue. All efforts to induce her were not successful, and a Cesarean delivery was required. (It is interesting how the mother's wish was fulfilled. Afraid of labor pains throughout the pregnancy she had wished to deliver the baby by Cesarean section.) Alicia was an early talker and walker, articulating words at eight months, and walking at nine months. She has had a smooth and uneventful physical development since then. What is she like at age three?

To begin with, she is very shy. When I first met Alicia, she responded to my questions only in a whisper. When I visited the family home, she remained upstairs hiding from me. "She went through the terrible two's," her mother explained. She used to be outgoing, Mrs. Gibson related, but then, around age two, she started to be afraid of strangers and is only now beginning to outgrow that fear. While an easy child overall, she is fearful of new situations, Mrs. Gibson explained. She is also very sensitive and a perfectionist. But she is also persistent, independent, dependable, generous, and generally cheerful. Mr. Gibson characterized Alicia as obstinate.

Since no other children live in their neighborhood, Alicia has spent most of her life in the company of adults—her mother, father, and grandmother. A month before I started interviewing the family, when Alicia was thirty-four months old, she was enrolled in a playgroup that met twice a week, for two hours a session. Once a week, every Sunday, she gets to play with her cousins, but otherwise, she keeps herself busy with a variety of activities. For instance, she likes to "help" her mother clean the house, wash the dishes, work in the garden, and bake. When not helping her mother, she is engaged in "doing her own things," such as building with Lego and Little-Village blocks or cutting, pasting, and playing with dolls. She has also enjoyed doing puzzles from an early age. At eighteen months, for example, she could complete an eight-piece puzzle; at twenty-four months, a twenty-piece puzzle; and at thirty-six months, a sixty-piece puzzle. She was never interested in rattles and other "regular" toys, but was always attracted to toys that "made her think," recounted Mrs. Gibson.

As the child of two music-loving and education-minded parents, one would expect music to have had some impact on Alicia. And indeed, music is one of her favorite activities, according to her parents. She likes to listen to them play the tuba and the clarinet, and enjoys listening to recordings of instrumental classical music, which is her parents' favorite music. She loves to sing, "singing all the time," related Mrs. Gibson. And since the age of twenty-nine months, she has been taking violin lessons by the Suzuki method with both mother and daughter enjoying the joint activity. To balance all of these activities with something more physical, Alicia has been given swimming lessons since she was thirty months old. What a busy life for a child not yet three years old! Where was the time to develop her early reading ability?

Taking a careful second look at Alicia's daily schedule, the question that comes to mind is, Is this schedule really significantly busier than the schedules of other children of similar age, or does it only appear to be so? Could it be that Alicia's life was more streamlined, organized, and carefully enriched, with more active and individualized adult attention given to her, than the lives of other preschoolers? After all, most children keep busy with a variety of activities. But who is to judge? Sometimes I feel that raising a young child is like raising a beautiful flower. Some parents give it a little time and some give it a great deal of time. Some tend to their child primarily once a day and some spend with him or her every free moment, lavishing on the child their thoughts and emotions. One can certainly say that Alicia's mother spent a great deal of time with her, having made a conscientious effort to give her the best that she could—facilitating her development as much as she could—during the early formative years.

In fact, both Gibsons believed that this attention was important for Alicia's overall development, and they made financial sacrifice for that purpose. It appears that the mother was content with her decision, and the child was thriving. (Alicia's apparent shyness and fear of strangers, which is not uncommon at her age, may be attributed to an innate temperamental trait she will outgrow once her social skills develop.)

HOW WELL DID ALICIA READ?

Before we examine Alicia's reading development, let us first find out how well she could actually read. Entering the testing room with her mother, Alicia approached my desk in a stride immediately setting herself to the reading task, while Mrs. Gibson settled next to her. The book with the six sentences lay open on the desk and I asked Alicia if she could read the title word (*Children*). There was no response. I opened the page with the first sentence and asked her to read that. Again, she did not respond. The second page with the second sentence received the same silent reaction. Mrs. Gibson interrupted, saying that if the sentences were written in lowercase, Alicia would probably be able to read them. I decided to give it a try, and wrote the sentences in lowercase on a sheet of paper. In a whispering voice, Alicia then proceeded to read each sentence, to her mother.

She read the first sentence fluently with no mistakes. She read the second sentence fluently. When she came to the third sentence, she made one error reading *boy* instead of the text's *baby*. We talked about the illustrations of the fourth and fifth sentences and she then read them fluently. The sixth sentence presented some difficulty with the word *she*, and I was not sure that Alicia had pronounced the second syllable of the word *going*. But Mrs. Gibson said that she had.

While certainly less fluent compared with the other children that were assessed, Alicia did meet, at thirty-five months, the reading criterion for admittance to the study. She was reading, as her father said, "haltingly," but she was able to read short, simple, and unfamiliar sentences, using different strategies when facing a difficult word. She would either sound out the word, ask one of her parents for help, or substitute another word with similar letters, explained Mr. Gibson.

HOW DID ALICIA LEARN TO READ?

How did this thirty-five-month-old girl acquire the ability to read that is usually associated with much older children? Some would say the answer is obvious: with two educator parents who valued early reading, and a mother who gave up an established teaching career in order to be at home full time with her preschooler, "the mother had probably taught her," they argued. Others may even add that Alicia's mother had pushed the child to justify her own resignation from her teaching career. Whatever the case may be, and irrespective of the parents' professional background and acknowledged role in Alicia's reading development, the Gibsons' literacy interactions with Alicia turned out to be quite similar to print interactions in the other homes of early readers that were studied.

As mentioned earlier, many, if not most, of these print interactions occurred incidentally, unsystematically, and embedded in Alicia's routine daily activities, inside or outside of the house. All the reading knowledge she acquired, whether it involved a basic concept (that words are constructed with letters, for example) or a skill (such as memorizing the sounds of the letters), occurred spontaneously. There was no prescribed formal teaching methodology to follow, nor was there any systematic approach to the Gibsons work with Alicia. Their only guideline was Alicia's interest and ability level, coupled with their strong desire to promote her development—not just in reading but in all aspects of her growth—as best as they could. Once Alicia showed some interest in print, the Gibsons actively sought out ways to stimulate that interest and encourage its development.

To better understand the nature of the Gibsons' print interactions with Alicia and the developmental process she experienced, let us look at the collection of anecdotes that her parents related. These anecdotes, which are arranged chronologically, describe Alicia's reading behavior, which begins before she was one year old.

At three months, Alicia's grandmother gave her a set of plastic alphabet blocks. At five months, Mrs. Gibson began to expose Alicia to *Sesame Street*. She had been interested in the program herself and started to watch it while nursing Alicia. She recalls how the baby would look up at the screen from time to time. At about six months, the parents started reading to Alicia from picture books. She had a couple of cloth books and many Golden Picture books, and she showed a great interest in the pictures, they recall. But actual interest in the stories developed only later, they say, when she was about nine months old. A snapshot taken at that time shows Alicia fully engrossed in a story read to her by her grandmother. There is nothing unique in these few facts. This type of literacy experience is common in homes of many preschool children. And nothing here could explain Alicia's early reading development.

By ten months, Alicia could recognize the word *Bert* on a Sesame Street poster, Mrs. Gibson recounted, and she enjoyed playing with a set of lotto alphabet cards. Intent to encourage her development, the parents decided to start buying developmentally appropriate picture books—to correspond with the *Sesame Street* television program she liked to watch—and by twelve months they gave her the book *Who Am I?* of that series. That book turned out to be her favorite reading material for a while, and they had to read it to Alicia repeatedly for a period of several months.

A is for Apple, B is for Bird

Since the family believed that early stimulation is important, a cousin gave Alicia a Sesame Street alphabet book when she was fourteen months old. She had been exposed to the letters for months by now, and was able to identify some of the letters right away, recalled the Gibsons. Impressed by her ability and eager to further develop it, they decided to encourage Alicia to learn the rest of the alphabet. And they approached the matter playfully, figuring this would be the only viable way to reach Alicia at her tender age and maintain her interest. For example, they would show her a letter and name it for her, expecting her to repeat it after them. Or they would call out a word, one word for each letter, saying: "*A* is for apple," "*B* is for Bert," "*C* is for cat," and so forth. Sometimes they would ask Alicia to identify a specific letter, "Where is *P* for Papa?" or "Where is *K* for kiss?" At other times, they would point at a letter and ask Alicia to name it for them. In another favorite game they would say, "Here is an *A*, What comes next?" and Alicia would be challenged to find the letter *B* in the pile of letters. Only uppercase letters were used in those early letter games, Mrs. Gibson recalled. And "Alicia loved to name the letters," she added.

"When she just 'passed' the alphabet book, Alicia started to recognize some storefront names." But "overall, word knowledge and letter knowledge were developed at the same time from both directions," Mr. Gibson explained. She learned to recognize a growing number of words while at the same time continuing to improve her letter knowledge. Most of the learning situations occurred naturally, spontaneously, and incidentally—during stimulating family play periods, during walks in the neighborhood, during shopping trips, and during her play activities with the many reading-related toys, games, and books she had. She had four different sets of letter cards, for example, with which she would often play, and these greatly improved her letter knowledge, recounted the Gibsons. *Sesame Street*, which she started watching three times a day, for the full three hours, has also contributed to her letter and word knowledge. And so have her favorite books, which had to be read to her several times a day, her parents said.

By the time she was eighteen months old, Alicia knew all the letters of the alphabet, in uppercase. Mrs. Gibson would often make a pile with the block letters and ask Alicia to pick out one letter or another. While the interaction was always playful, it was also useful to find out which letters Alicia knew and which still needed to be worked on, Mrs. Gibson explained. By eighteen months, she could identify all the letters without making a single mistake.

By that time Alicia could also recall from memory several favorite stories, the stories that had been read to her repeatedly, and she would occasionally enjoy telling these stories to her parents. She loved to show off her ability, they say, and bask in their compliments. (The parents saw some correlation between Alicia's reading development and her puzzle work, recalling that by eighteen months she could also assemble seven- and eight-piece puzzles.)

Up to this point, the driving force behind most of the print interactions between Alicia and her parents sprang from the Gibsons' desire to stimulate and encourage their child's development, combined, of course, with Alicia's inborn curiosity and desire to learn. These two basic desires are probably instinctive and common in many parents–child dyads. They are probably innate to the species and, in fact, the basis for all human development, in all cultures and throughout history. However, what is missing in many children's homes, particularly when it comes to the issue of early reading development, is the insight into what is possible; that is, what young children are actually capable of doing. Consequently, as addressed in Chapter 2, there has been a lowered level of expectation and a decreased level of encouragement and stimulation of early literacy.

Many parents simply followed the conventional twentieth-century notion: that children younger than age six lack the ability to learn to read. And because of that common notion, most parents have not even tried to encourage that development. Even if they thought their preschooler was mentally ready to grasp the mechanics of reading (or parts of it), the parents were often intimidated into not doing anything about it (the child is too young, you may harm him or her by too much pressure or too early stimulation, and so on). Other parents lacked the time or patience to facilitate their children's reading development. In any case, Alicia's parents were free of all of these inhibitions and they did not shy away from stimulating their child's literacy development.

Glen Doman's Influence

When Alicia was nineteen months old, Mrs. Gibson saw a television program that dramatically impacted her attitude toward early reading, and her resolution to facilitate Alicia's early development. She was surfing the channels, she says, when she came across an interview with Glen Doman, the controversial author-educator of *How to Teach Your Baby to Read.* And she was hooked, she says. If she had been positively disposed toward early reading to begin with, she was now convinced that this was possible. She was so impressed by the mental achievements of the babies demonstrated in Doman's interview that she determined to try to achieve some level of early reading ability with Alicia. "If these babies could be stimulated to such a degree, there is no reason I couldn't do the same with Alicia," she thought. In addition, she felt that Doman's approach to infant stimulation would provide her with another way of interacting with Alicia—on a much deeper and intimate level than is the norm. "After all, there is a limit to puzzles and shapes," she added. Following that television interview with Glen Doman, Mrs. Gibson read his book, adopting some of his recommendations, and incorporating them with her other spontaneous, incidental, print interactions with Alicia.

By the time Alicia was twenty months old, she was able to recall from memory *Bears in the Night* by Jan and Stan Bernstain, her favorite storybook at the time, and she began to pretend "reading" that book aloud to her parents, pointing at each word. Observing her impressive progress, the Gibsons wondered how they could further develop Alicia's ability, and they decided to give her a set of magnetic alphabet letters and a board for Christmas. She already knew all the letters, they say, and they figured she would soon want to make some words with the letters. The magnetic letters would be perfect for that purpose, they thought. Soon thereafter, Mrs. Gibson casually started to spell simple words on that board, leaving the words on for the day, to be viewed by Alicia. And Alicia would watch as her mother spelled the words on the board.

Intuitively considering Alicia's reading development to be a natural process that had some intrinsic logic, the Gibsons thought it would be wise at that point (as they were getting ready for spelling) to draw Alicia's attention to lowercase letters. "This is a capital *A* and this is a small *a*," they'd tell Alicia. "This is a capital *B* and this is a small *b*," and so on. They sensed she was ready for that step, and they expected she would understand the difference between uppercase and lowercase letters. And she did. From then on, it was only a matter of practice, through play, until the child would have a solid knowledge of the difference between uppercase and lowercase letters. To keep her engaged, the Gibsons tried their best to make each print interaction with Alicia as entertaining and stimulating as possible, they recounted.

Word Games

By January, when she was twenty-two months old, Mrs. Gibson bought for Alicia a new *Sesame Street* book titled *I Can Do It Myself*. Following Doman's recommendation, she did not give her the book right away. She first prepared cards, one card for each word in that book (a total of forty cards), and she then started giving Alicia two or three cards per day, naming the words for her. Several weeks later, she increased the rate to four words per day, she related. Whenever Alicia was able to read a number of these words, she would be rewarded with stickers, one sticker for every word. Once she could read a full sentence, Mrs. Gibson would print that sentence on a piece of tag board and place it on the refrigerator. The sentences started to accumulate on the refrigerator, Mrs Gibson recalled.

And so the days passed at the Gibson household, one day following another, peacefully, predictably, with little Alicia singing all over the house and keeping herself busy with a variety of activities: emulating her mother's household chores, tagging along on shopping trips, watching *Sesame Street*, playing a few word-and-letter games, listening to a story or two, or engaging herself with puzzles, Legos, or some of her other many toys. For Valentine's Day, the Gibsons gave Alicia a new book titled *Grover's New Kitten*, another Sesame Street publication that would become a favorite. That book had to be read to her daily, and within a month, she could recite it from memory to her parents' delight. Often, she would pretend to read the book, pointing at the words. They were amazed with her ability, they recall. And each book they gave her made the following books easier, because Alicia would remember a few new words from each new book and was able to recognize them in the following books. She had a good visual memory for words, Mrs. Gibson recounted.

Was Alicia's ability to recognize words at the age of twenty-two months innate? Or was it developed through the many word-and-letter games her parents played with her? We will never know. What we do know from recent brain research, is that the brain is very plastic in the early years: the more it is activated, the more the neural system develops, and the more connections are formed between brain cells. This enriched activity leads to a more extended mental brain capacity. (This point is further discussed in Chapter 10.)

By April, when Alicia was two years old—some four months after her parents started playing with her the cards for *I Can Do It Myself*—she could read all the words of that book, they recalled. The Gibsons then gave her that book. She was able to read through it right away, and the sentences were taken off the refrigerator. New words appeared on the refrigerator, and in family games. And as Alicia's awareness of words increased, she slowly started to recognize words in newspapers and magazines, her parents recalled.

Rhyme and Sound Games

But then the Gibsons began to worry. They were concerned, they say, that Alicia's ability to recognize isolated words would not be enough to develop a fluent reading capability, and that she would soon forget the words. So they started to grope for a way to better facilitate her reading development. Intuitively, they decided to give her clusters of rhyming words—*mop, hop, top,* or *pig, dig, big,* for instance—hoping that a developed sense for rhyming would help her reading fluency. And they did something else. They decided to develop her phonetic awareness by playing a variety of sound games with her: "*S* sounds like s-s-s-s-snake," they'd say. "*B* sounds like b-b-b-b-bee," "*D* sounds like d-d-d-d-dog," and so on. They figured, intuitively, that knowing the sounds of the letters would help her reading. Also Sesame Street was very useful in that respect, they recalled, providing a large display of sound games with tips on how to present them to preschool children. Alicia was like a sponge, said the Gibsons, absorbing all this new information.

The following summer, when Alicia was twenty-seven months old, mother and daughter started taking weekly trips to the public library. Mrs. Gibson would check out a few books for Alicia and Alicia would select a book or two by herself. "She tended to choose books she had already seen before," Mrs. Gibson related.

Within a few months of playing the sound games, Alicia knew the sounds of the whole alphabet. And what did she do with that knowledge? She began to "break words into letters," recalled her mother. To strengthen her decoding ability, one of the Gibsons would pronounce short rhyming words and ask Alicia to name their letters. Another sounding-out game, for example, was something like "*B* stands for *Bert*, buh-buh-buh . . . what other words sound like that?" Or "*K* stands for kiss k-k-k . . . what other words sound like that?" Grocery advertisements soon provided another means to practice sounding out words. And as Mrs. Gibson would prepare her grocery lists, Alicia would often make her own list (with her mother's help), mirroring her mother. "It is a fun time for both of us," Mrs. Gibson remarked. By the time she was thirty-four months old, Alicia got so involved with sounding out words, her mother remarked, that "whenever she sees a word, she must sound it out to its components." But "there is a difference in her reading now," Mrs. Gibson added. "Until now she used to read only whole words she could recognize, but now she is beginning to sound out even difficult new words."

There were many other print-related activities in the Gibson home. The family was so literacy-oriented that almost any activity they engaged in could be turned into some reading or writing event. For example, when they would be in the car during a family trip, Mrs. Gibson would write on a "magic" slate whatever Alicia would say and then hold the slate up and ask Alicia to read the words. Once she read the words, the mother would erase the slate and write some new material, until both mother and child got tired.

Letters to Grandma

Letters to grandma became another favorite learning experience. Alicia would tell her mother what she wanted to write and Mrs. Gibson would help her with the spelling as she printed the words with a pencil on a lined notebook paper. GRANDMA AND GRANDPA, THE MAILMAN BROUGHT ME STICKERS. THANK YOU. LOVE ALICIA,

was one such letter her mother showed me. Alicia wrote that letter when she was almost three, Mrs. Gibson related, and the
twelve words were sprawled over two standard notebook
pages—with their size ranging from tiny to an inch and one-half
tall, but this did not matter to Alicia or her mother. Soon Alicia
would start spelling short easy words by herself. She would also
copy words from books with her pencil. And once she showed an
interest in copying words, the Gibsons started buying all the
reading readiness workbooks and connect-the-dot coloring
books of letters and numbers they could find. Alicia enjoyed
these workbooks, they recalled.

When I last saw Alicia, she was thirty-six months old. Her
favorite book at the time was *Little Bunny Follows His Nose* by
Katherine Howard. This book had to be read to her daily, often
several times. She could read it by herself about halfway through
but then would get tired and need some assistance. Mrs. Gibson
would patiently help her—articulating the difficult words or
sounding them out with her.

IN A NUTSHELL

This chronology of events illustrates how one developmental step followed another. Deeply in tune with Alicia, the Gibsons
could always sense the level of Alicia's print awareness, and they
tried their best to further stimulate and promote her reading interest. Approaching the process intuitively and with much logic,
they would develop her ability from any direction that would
make sense to them, careful all along to match Alicia's capability
with interesting and challenging activities.

Although Mrs. Gibson acknowledged her active role in Alicia's reading development, it is interesting to note that this child
experienced a learning process that turned out to be quite similar to that of Sean, Carrie, and Brian. It appears that here, too, a
natural learning process emerged, based on Alicia's innate curiosity and desire to learn, and her parents' drive to stimulate
and promote that development. While this process was natural
and unsystematic, it had an intrinsic logic. And once the data
was carefully analyzed, a distinct pattern of reading development emerged.

First, there was a preliminary period of gaining rudimentary print awareness, which included, in Alicia's case, an exposure to *Sesame Street*, playing with alphabet blocks and cards, and listening to her parents' daily readings. Some attention was also given to printed words in the environment, before she was one year old.

At fourteen months, there was a change in Alicia's behavior toward print. After she received an alphabet book, her parents started playing with her a variety of letter games, with a conscientious effort to encourage her letter knowledge. Continuously demonstrating her interest in print, she also began to acquire, in parallel, and with her parents' encouragement, some sight vocabulary. She started watching *Sesame Street* intensely, often three times a day.

About six months later, at the age of twenty months (while continuing to improve her letter knowledge and build up her sight vocabulary), Alicia began to "read" to her parents, word by word, from books that had been read to her before. At twenty-five months, the Gibsons started to play sound games with Alicia. By thirty-two months, she began to show an interest in spelling and writing, and enjoyed printing words. At thirty-three months, Mrs. Gibson practiced with Alicia sounding-out games, and by thirty-four months, she started to sound out unfamiliar words by herself. Increasingly, Alicia's readings to her parents reflected a true reading capability rather than a recall from memory of familiar text.

This sequence of reading development indicates the existence of several steps or stages in that development. As discussed in the earlier accounts of Sean, Carrie, and Brian, each of these stages was characterized by a distinct reading behavior, involving a particular reading concept, on which Alicia would focus and practice for a period of several months—until she reached a zone of comfortable proficiency. Once she felt sufficiently competent in the particular skill of a given stage, her interest would shift (with her parent's help) to a new phase, involving a new reading concept and skill necessary to achieve full reading capability. These stages can be summarized as follows:

Stage 1: Alicia gained general awareness of books and print (ongoing at five months).

Stage 2: Alicia learned to identify the letters and began to acquire a sight vocabulary (starting at fourteen months).

Stage 3: Alicia began to "read" aloud to her parents (from twenty months).

Stage 4: Alicia learned the sounds of the letters (starting at twenty-five months).

Stage 5: Alicia showed interest in spelling and printing words (starting at thirty-two months).

Stage 6: Alicia started to sound out by herself unfamiliar words (starting at thirty-four months).

THE PARENTS' ROLE IN ALICIA'S READING DEVELOPMENT

Would Alicia have become an early reader without her parents help? Probably not. But believing, as they did, that the early years of childhood are a period of rapid growth that should not be "wasted," is there any surprise that they helped bring out Alicia's ability? The Gibsons derived tremendous satisfaction from their child's reading development. And once the mother noticed the child's budding interest and joy in learning, she was even more determined to encourage that development. She also considered it to be her responsibility. Besides, Mrs. Gibson had a deep desire to create a special relationship with her child—a more unique relationship than the typical mother–daughter bond—and she thought that by helping Alicia learn to read before formal schooling, she would achieve that special bond.

And so, taking their parenting roles seriously, both parents strove to give Alicia the best upbringing they were capable of, which included, in their view, early literacy stimulation. And unlike some other parents, Mrs. Gibson does acknowledge her active role in her daughter's development. It is interesting to note, therefore, how Alicia's parents still wisely chose the natural process. They could have followed some prescribed standardized instructional methodology, but they chose instead the more simple, intuitive, flexible, spontaneous, and unsystematic approach, which they felt was more suited for a child of Alicia's age. This approach was also more enjoyable for both parents and child.

Like the other parents portrayed in this book, the Gibsons sensitively based their literacy interactions with Alicia on the child's interests, curiosity, and level of ability. Using a variety of didactic techniques, which they adapted from books and educational television programs or creatively invented themselves, they helped Alicia learn the names of the letters and acquire a sight vocabulary. They coached her with the sounds of the letters and encouraged her with spelling, they guided her with workbooks, and read with her daily, pointing at the words. And they turned many of their print interactions with Alicia into reading games, to make the learning process an enjoyable, fun-filled experience. But perhaps the most important element in Alicia's early literacy development was the Gibsons' true enjoyment in opening their child's eyes and mind to the world of print, whenever that was possible.

Chapter Seven

A Four-Year-Old Reader at Second-Grade Level

To avoid parting with his collection of 117,000 books while traveling, the avid reader and Grand Vizier of Persia, Abdul Kassem Ismael (c. 1000 A.D.), has them carried by a caravan of four hundred camels.
—Alberto Manguel, *A History of Reading*

THE CILANO FAMILY

Let us now visit the home of John Cilano, who was identified as an early reader when he was three years, one month old. Not realizing at first that their son's reading development was accelerated, it took a family friend, a professional speech therapist, to draw the Cilanos' attention to that. And once their eyes were opened, they were awash with pride mixed with deep concern. What was the reason for their anxiety? How did it affect John's reading development? Let us take a closer look at John and his home environment.

The Cilanos live in a large eastern city, in a comfortable eighty-year-old house located in a middle-class neighborhood. The family includes the father, thirty-three, the mother, thirty-one, and one brother, Adam, who is two years younger than John. The parents are natives who grew up in the city, but John was born in New York City and lived there until age one and a half when his parents decided to return home and open their own business.

The family is extended with paternal grandparents, maternal grandmother, and several maternal aunts all living in the area. Being the only grandchildren and nephews in that family, John and Adam are the focus of much adult attention. One aunt in particular, an early reader herself, is especially fond of John, and she spends a great deal of time playing and reading with him, Mrs. Cilano recounted.

Mr. Cilano is a jack-of-all-trades person, according to his wife. He has a degree and work experience in accounting, but when the company he used to work for wanted to transfer him abroad, he decided to teach himself computer skills, became a computer analyst, and opened up his own business. Mrs. Cilano used to be a chef in a French restaurant but became a full-time mother when John was born. She now works in the evenings as a beauty consultant for a national company. She does not like to leave the children with a sitter, she says, and plans to work on a more regular basis only when the children are in school full time.

Both parents are attentive to John, but as the father is often out of town on business trips, the mother feels she has the major responsibility for raising the children. During the weekends, however, when Mr. Cilano is at home, the boys are reportedly his treat. He enjoys spending a great deal of time with John, Mrs. Cilano relates, reading, playing print-related games, and answering his many questions.

The Cilanos are avid readers, they say, and they had always wished that John would also grow to like books. Mr. Cilano "likes to book shop," and he brings new books to John whenever he returns home from out of town. "Golden Books were at home even before John was born," the mother remarked. Still, both parents related independently that they never intended to teach John to read. He had an "innate ability to read. We nurtured it, but it was inside him," Mrs. Cilano explained. "John taught himself to read, but *Sesame Street* was instrumental and so was our interest," added Mr. Cilano.

But now that John knows how to read, his parents have mixed feelings about it. Although helpful all along in developing his ability, and quite proud of it, the Cilanos feel overwhelmed and somewhat burdened by the responsibility this puts on them. The mother, in particular, feels John's early reading ability presents a problem for them, being basically alone in their search for the best way to manage and develop it. She also worries about problems that may develop in the future, wondering "How will the [school] system react to his developed talent?"

This sense of heavy burden, almost distress, with which this family responds to John's early reading ability can be better understood with some background of Mrs. Cilano's experience with her sister. She, too, was an early reader. But today, at age thirty, while still a very bright person, she is considered by the family to be a wasted talent. She twice earned a scholarship for college and dropped out. She does not work, still lives with her mother, and "is doing nothing, absolutely nothing," John's mother lamented. This sister's failure follows Mrs. Cilano like a shadow, tormenting her with the possibility of a similar fate for John. No special effort was made to develop her sister's talent, Mrs. Cilano explained. And she strongly feels, therefore, that they must actively do something to facilitate John's mental as well as emotional development, to prevent him from coming to a fate similar to that of his aunt.

PORTRAIT OF ANOTHER NATURAL READER

Slender, fine featured, with smooth brown hair and large expressive blue eyes, John gets flashes of mercurial intensity and strong facial expressions that swing in mood from mild anxiety to a relaxed mischievous smile. He was an early walker and talker, walking at eight months and articulating words at six months and sentences at about a year, relates his mother. His pronunciation was clear and correct from the start, his father added.

He is not an easy child, confides his mother. John is extremely sensitive and active, she says. He is intense in his emotions and often moody, "an excessive compulsive" who "does not bend well to rules," she added. Otherwise, he is persistent, a perfectionist, fearful of new situations, competitive, curious, dependable, driven, and possesses a good memory. John's social interactions at this point are limited to children in his nursery school and to his younger brother, of whom he is still a bit jealous, recounted Mrs. Cilano, not yet fully accepting him as part of the family. He likes to interact with adults, or play alone with his small plastic animals (dinosaurs are the latest attraction), and read. "He is not a toy person," his mother remarked, never having been interested in trucks or other typical toys for children of his age. To release excessive energy, he will often race around the house, and run up and down the stairs, she added.

The parents say that reading is John's favorite activity. Having never scribbled, his first attempts with a pencil were deliberately for the purpose of writing the letters of the alphabet. But he now likes to draw and paint and to sing and make up his own songs (he learns new songs easily). He has been taking violin lessons by the Suzuki method since age three—"to give him something to do"—Mrs. Cilano explained, but he does not like it: "It has been work for him, and he fights it." He does not like repetition and gets easily bored, she added, admitting that she, too, found the sessions wearing.

HOW DID JOHN LEARN TO READ?

So how did John learn to read if his parents had never intended to teach him? His intelligence level and verbal ability, as measured by the two popular tests, are indeed far above average. His standard score on the Peabody Picture Vocabulary Test, given at age four years, five months, was 153 (ninety-ninth percentile). His IQ score on the Stanford Binet Intelligence Scale, administered at the same age, was 140. Both scores are high. But we know that a high score on intelligence tests does not necessarily lead to an early reading development. Moreover, children with a low IQ score can also become early readers. So there must be another explanation for John's early reading development.

Did television play some role in John's literacy development? He likes to watch television, his parents admitted, spending between two to three hours a day viewing a variety of programs. His exposure to *Sesame Street* started on his mother's lap when he was barely a few weeks old, she says. She liked to watch the program, getting insight on how to interact with children, and she noticed that John was "soaking things up."

Then from the age of fifteen months until he was three, he would watch the program daily, she says, and later on, he continued to view the program occasionally with his brother. While his favorite programs at age four years, six months were *Electric Company* and *Mr. Rogers' Neighborhood*, *Sesame Street* was instrumental in contributing to John's letter knowledge and sight vocabulary, according to Mr. Cilano. Yet, many children watch *Sesame Street* every day and do not learn to read early. So there must be another reason for John's early development.

JOHN'S EXPERIENCE WITH PRESCHOOL

Did John learn to read in preschool? The summer before he turned three (at thirty-four months), the Cilanos did enroll John in a preschool program. Since there were no other children in their neighborhood, they wanted to expose him to children of his age and provide him with a positive experience away from the baby at home. He was placed in a summer playgroup at the local community center. He had a good time there, his mother recounted, but she felt the place was too play-oriented for him.

The following September, at age three, John was enrolled in a Montessori nursery school. The Cilanos thought this program would be more mentally stimulating for John, Mrs. Cilano explained. One of the teachers reportedly told them that "John could read words around the classroom" at the beginning of the school year, and that he was particularly fond of two alphabet puzzles. He would spend most of his time there working alone on these puzzles, or he would carry them around in his pockets, verbalizing about them. But there was no direct attempt to facilitate John's reading development in that setting, Mrs. Cilano explained. Moreover, that Montessori program was too structured for John, and he had a very hard time adjusting to the rules and regulations of the place. "It was a trial for him," Mrs. Cilano recalled. "He wanted to have full control of the situation and lay down the rules." The parents decided to look for another program for John.

At age four, he was placed in a newly opened program at a private school for the gifted. He was an independent reader by then, related Mrs. Cilano. And while the teachers gave him as much individualized attention as he needed, the mother continued to be unhappy with their choice—not sure if that was the right place for John, and if that program was worth its high cost. For kindergarten, the Cilanos decided to reenroll John at the Montessori school, but the program was full by then. And so the family's final decision was to keep John at the school for the gifted for another year. This way his mother, at least, had the peace of mind they were doing all that was possible to facilitate John's development. So how, where, and when did John learn to read? Before we examine his reading development, let us find out how well John could actually read.

HOW WELL DID JOHN READ?

John's ability to read the six criterion sentences was first observed on campus, when he was thirty-seven months old. The full extent of his reading ability was informally assessed when I started my study, during one of my visits to the Cilanos' home. He was then forty-eight months old. I asked John to read selections from a number of readers. He read fluently, with no mistakes, several pages from preprimers in an old copy I had of *Graded Selections for Informal Diagnosis* by Nila Banton Smith. I then showed him the Macmillan basal readers, and he asked me to start reading to him from each story I would show him. I agreed. And so I would start the story and read a few sentences, and then he would continue to read several sentences, until I would ask him to stop. He read fluently, with no errors, several sentences from "Izzy" in the Macmillan primer. He read fluently several sentences from "Little Blue and Little Yellow," and "The Song of Little Frog," in the First Reader. He then read a number of sentences from "Sticks, Stones" in the Second Reader. At this point he started to change several *the* words to *a* words. And twice, when he came across an unfamiliar name, he stopped reading as if waiting for me to help him out. (I later found out that at home this was his typical reaction to a difficult word whenever an adult was with him.) When I asked him to sound out these words, he would do that and then continue his reading.

I felt that John had the ability to continue to read in the Third Reader, but he began to tire and started to lose interest. The pictures in the book also started to distract him (perhaps because I kept moving him from one story to another before he had a chance to get the full content). So I decided to stop the assessment at that point. Without trying to formally assess his comprehension level, there was little doubt, judging from the questions that John asked, that he had good overall understanding of the text he was reading.

Furthermore, the day he was administered the Peabody Picture Vocabulary Test, I had another chance to informally observe John's reading ability. He had brought along his *The Children's Bible*, his favorite book at the time, and while we were waiting for the tester to arrive, he asked me to read to him the chapter about Samson and Delilah. I did. He then continued to read another portion. Very interested in the complicated plot, he started to half read, half skim the text to get as quickly as possible the overall content, and then (perhaps because of growing fatigue), he started skimming the page for keywords. There was no sounding out of difficult words. He was so eager to get the story, he did not even want to bother with the slow mechanics of the reading task, getting out of the story, through keywords, as much as he was able to comprehend.

In brief, I concluded that at the age of four years, seven months, John was a fluent reader of at least second-grade level, with apparently good comprehension ability for that level. He also showed a fair technical ability, and desire, to read from text that was largely above his comprehension level (as, for example, the chapter about Samson and Delilah). "He certainly reads much that he does not understand," his father concurred, including the *Sunday New York Times*. Some of his favorite books at age four and a half are *The Children's Bible*, a Golden Press book; *The Golden Book Encyclopedia Series*; and a picture dictionary (with fifteen hundred words). He liked to read in these books by himself, his parents related, and also have others read to him from them, they added.

CHRONOLOGY OF EVENTS

So how did John acquire this level of reading ability? There is nothing about his personality that would dramatically distinguish him from other children of similar age and explain his early reading development. True, he had an exceptionally high IQ score, but this does not explain an early reading ability, nor is it a prerequisite for natural reading development. His mother's traumatic experience with her sister (the perceived failure to live up to her intellectual potential) may have cast a shadow on the Cilano's household, causing Mrs. Cilano to be especially sensitive and anxious about John's mental and emotional development. This distress—evident from the constant change of preschool programs—may have contributed to the parents' desire to provide John with a highly literate home and school environment. Yet, the parents honestly maintain that John learned to read by himself; that he had an innate ability for reading and they only nurtured it—intuitively, spontaneously—helping out, as they said, day in, day out.

So what was the nature of his spontaneous nonsystematic reading development? To get better insight, we will now take a closer look at a sample of John's print-related behavior, beginning with his first year of life. This sample, which is arranged chronologically, was taken from a collection of anecdotes his parents related during a series of retrospective interviews regarding John's reading development.

When he was just a few weeks old, Mrs. Cilano started to expose John to *Sesame Street* while nursing him. He used to stare at the screen from time to time, she recalled, as she was watching the program.

Flipping through Books

At six months he started to show an interest in books and magazines. He used to flip through books, chew the books, rip them, and overall find "good amusement" in doing that, Mrs. Cilano recalled. So the parents gave him his very own first cloth book, titled *Teddy Bear*, the first book that could be safely left with him without fear of being ripped or chewed apart.

They would read to John daily from Golden Books that lay around the house. They had "always" read to him, the mother reflected, "even when I breast-fed him." His father used to read to him at bedtime, she added. Overall, the parents' readings during those early months were a whole language experience, Mrs.

Cilano explained, including pointing at and looking at the pictures, talking about the pictures, reading the print around those pictures while pointing at the words, building up a vocabulary, and learning to articulate the words. At eight months John received a set of alphabet blocks.

When he was about one year old, John wanted to keep his *Teddy Bear* cloth book always with him, recalled Mrs. Cilano, and he would take it along wherever they would go. He would constantly turn the pages and ask to be read from it. He liked to make up stories about the pictures in that book, she said. All in all, he made so much use of that book that eventually it had to be discarded and another copy had to be purchased for him, his mother related. Another favorite book at the time, a beautifully illustrated sturdy book with one rhyming sentence per page, was *Out in the Woods* by Rose Art Studios. That book was also read to John repeatedly, often several times a day, recalled the mother.

Recognizing Sign Words

At one year John could "read" several words, the parents related. These were primarily sign words such as *bus, stop,* and *exit,* which he had learned from *Sesame Street,* they say. At about the same period (twelve months), he also knew the names of most of the letters, having also learned these from *Sesame Street.* "But he didn't understand yet that letters are the building blocks of words," remarked Mr. Cilano. "He realized that words were words before he knew the alphabet." The mother related that by twelve months John would often try to arrange his letter blocks by order of the alphabet. (The parents probably encouraged this behavior with their modeling and interest.)

Stimulated by John's active response to print, Mr. Cilano started bringing a "special" book for John whenever he returned from a business trip. John enjoyed these books, but *Teddy Bear* remained his favorite, and soon he knew it by heart, Mrs. Cilano recalled. "Between one and two he could read that book," remarked the father. At fourteen months he could also recite the whole alphabet, and he started his attempts to draw the letters with a pencil. (His first graphic attempts were letter-oriented, said Mrs. Cilano.) Another favorite book at the time was *Puppies* by Art Seiden. That book also had to be read to John daily, several times. Often, Mrs. Cilano would make rhymes with words in that book, she said, explaining she had "always liked to make silly songs and word games about everything" with John.

An Obsession with Letters

For Christmas, when he was fifteen months old, the Cilanos gave John a set of colorful magnetic letters (in uppercase) with a board. That gift had such a powerful impact on John and his reading development, that it could be divided into two periods: the premagnetic-letters period and the postmagnetic-letters period, explain the Cilanos.

"It was a deliberate decision to buy those letters for John," Mr. Cilano explained. Once he had observed that John could recognize several words, he wanted him to know "phonics." And he bought the magnetic letter set with that specific purpose in mind—to help John become more aware of the letters and their sounds. He thought this was important, because he had learned to read by the phonetic method and became a good reader, while a cousin who had learned to read by the whole word method has never liked to read, supposedly because of the "wrong" teaching methodology, explained Mr. Cilano. It was important to him, therefore, that John learn the letters and their sounds.

And, as it turned out, that magnetic-letter set started John's "obsession with the letters." Although he was used to playing with block letters, and occasionally even attempted to draw letters with a pencil before receiving the magnetic-letter set, he had never before been obsessed about letters. But once he had the magnetic letters, they became all-consuming, his parents said, and all he wanted to do was play with them.

His obsession was so strong that he started to make letters everywhere and with everything. For example, when the family would go to the beach and Mr. Cilano would start building something with sand, John wanted him only to draw letters in the sand. When he found a bunch of drinking straws, he wanted to make letters with them. When working with Play Dough, he would only make letters. Soup with alphabet noodles, which used to be a favorite, became a disaster, his mother recalled. He would not touch it, she says, crying that he could not eat the letters. *W* in particular became John's favorite letter. "It was like his friend," explained Mr. Cilano, taking it along wherever he would go. (The parents had no explanation for John's obsession with letters, or his attachment to *W*, saying about the latter that he might have seen in it a fancy-looking *M* [his real name's first letter], turned upside down).

By that time, at fifteen months, John "really" started to watch *Sesame Street*, Mrs. Cilano recounted, and he began to view the program daily. He also started to trace his magnetic letters with a pencil. Slowly, his fascination with the shapes of letters led to a desire to know their names, and soon the family found itself immersed in a letter-naming binge, with John continually asking and naming the letters of the alphabet. "Within a couple of months," when he was about seventeen months old, he "knew all the letters' names, even when shown to him at random," Mrs. Cilano recalled. And then he started to learn their sounds, she said, with their help and encouragement. For example, one of the parents would ask John, "How does *J* sound?" And he would say "juh-juh-juh," or one would ask, "How does *P* sound?" and he would respond with "puh-puh-puh," and so on. His interest remained focused on the sounds of the letters for several months, and any letter-related question would be directed to their sounds. "It was like a game," Mrs. Cilano explained.

Forming Words

By the time he was about eighteen months old, John started a new letter activity: he began "to put the letters into words." For example, *Exit*, *Mom*, *Dad*, *John*, and *Wet Paint* (all words that were meaningful to him) were among the first words he tried to put together, his parents recalled. (It is immaterial who was first to initiate that activity, whether John or his parents. The important point is that he enjoyed this challenge.) "He would do it from his head," Mrs. Cilano explained. Sometimes he would try to sound out the word, or ask her "How do you spell . . . ?" At other times she would say to him, "Let's see if you can find your name," or "Let's see if you could write . . . ." It was another game between them, she reflected.

And at that period, when John started to form words, the Cilanos noticed that he began to be interested in the mechanics of reading, rather than just memorizing the words. It was as if he finally understood, conceptually, that the encoding process and the decoding process—that is, writing and reading—are two aspects of the same thing, each skill being the opposite of and dependent on the other.

A Favorite Game

All along his parents tried their best to be helpful to John and avail themselves whenever he had a print-related question or wish. They spent a great deal of time, they say, doing word and letter activities with him. A favorite game, for example, at that period, ran like this: if he would spell the word *in*, Mr. Cilano would take the letter *P* and "walk" or "dance" it to stand in front of *in*, challenging John to read the new word *Pin*, and so on. They were often impressed by his insistence on getting the exact answers to his particular questions. He would resist any attempt to interfere with or change the direction of his thought. "He knew what he wanted," Mr. Cilano remarked.

What could be the next step in this unsystematic reading development? Where would John's curiosity lead to now? And how would the family continue to encourage his development? At the age of twenty-two months, an aunt gave John a set of Sesame Street flash cards. Each of these cards had a picture of a Sesame Street character, with one word describing a concept, such as *Home, In, Out, Exit, Entrance*, and so forth. John enjoyed playing with these cards for many months, his mother recalled, learning about the different concepts while building up his sight vocabulary.

"When he was two he already knew how to read," remarked Mr. Cilano. One of his favorite books at the time was *Puppies, Pussy Cats and Other Friends* by Gyo, and he began to take an active part in his parents' daily readings to him, "helping" them read the words he could recognize, Mrs. Cilano recalled. Occasionally, depending on the book, he would want to read after them sentence by sentence, she said.

Becoming Possessive

And then, within a short time, "when he could read [in] a very limited way, John suddenly became possessive about his reading, and he did not want us to read much to him," recalled Mrs. Cilano. He would often get angry when they would read to him, she said. It was as if he felt reading was "his" domain, and he did not want them to interfere with it or help him. (It is also possible that he got irritated with their constant attempts to correct his errors. When I mentioned that possibility to the mother, she remarked, "Maybe that's why he doesn't want to read with me.") Occasionally he would come to one of his parents and ask them to read to him a particular story, but it was mostly his grandmother and aunt who would now read to him, related Mrs. Cilano; he never rebelled against them.

In any case, slowly buying books from the Sesame Street Library Series, the Cilanos gradually acquired the full twelve-volume set. These volumes included letter and number activities, stories about *Sesame Street* characters, many cartoons, fairy tales, nursery rhymes, games, and much more. John liked that series so much, his mother recalled, that for the following year and a half they would spend more time with these books than with any of his other many books. Thus, although "possessive" of his reading with them and reportedly not wanting his parents to read much to him, he still had, between his second and third year, quite a bit of reading activity with his parents every day.

For Christmas, when he was thirty months old, he received a Texas Instruments electronic toy with which he liked to play a lot. It involved letters and words and many spelling games that would challenge John. He also started to play Scrabble, excited to participate in a favorite family pastime. And, at thirty-one months, he knew the sounds of all the letters, and was able to spell without help simple words on his magnetic board, recalled Mrs. Cilano.

Slowly, John's interest in letters began to subside, and his obsession with letters, which started at fifteen months, diminished. He was three years old then, and as he was starting to read by himself, the letters became a secondary interest. Mrs. Cilano summed up that development, reflecting, "First he played with letters, then he made words, then he made sentences, and then he started to read. By the time he was three he was reading. Sometimes he faked reading, [he would] read a few words and faked others" depending on the degree of difficulty of the text.

A Subscription to a Children's Magazine

The year between ages three and four the parents got for John a subscription to *Sesame Street* magazine, which he enjoyed immensely, they say. His reading—including sounding out of unfamiliar words—became more fluent. There was a definite progression from the previous year, Mrs. Cilano noticed. He stopped to sound out new words letter by letter, and it was "as if he sounded it out in his head." Once he got the first syllable he may have guessed the rest of the word, she added.

Increasingly, reading became a private activity for John. Mrs. Cilano had to now spend more time with Adam, her younger child, and Mr. Cilano started traveling more often. But John was now ready to do his reading by himself, his mother related. He also started to write words with a pencil, writing by forty months *Vito*, the name of his grandfather. Although he had spelled that name many times before with his magnetic letters, it was a big day for John when he could write that name with a pencil, recalled his mother.

At four, he began to lose interest in the Sesame Street Library Series, and increasingly spent time reading by himself in the volumes of his *Golden Book Encyclopedia*, his mother related. He now loved to read to his parents. Instead of "helping" them in their readings to him, or taking turns alternating their readings—he reading a page then one of the parents reading the following page—he was now able to read a whole book to them.

Reading for Enjoyment of Content

Another noticeable change in John's reading behavior, around age four, had to do with his motivation for reading. Up until then, observed Mrs. Cilano, John's primary motivation for reading was his desire to master the technical skill of reading. "It was a mental game for him," Mr. Cilano added. First it was a game for himself and then it was a game with his parents. But around age four, he started to read for the enjoyment of content, they say, and for reference purposes. For example, when the family was planning a trip to Hawaii, John asked his father to tell him about the islands. Listening intently to his father's description of Hawaiian volcanoes, he became immensely interested in the topic. And later that day, Mr. Cilano found him reading aloud by himself, in his bedroom, the section in his encyclopedia about volcanoes.

But "there is a difference from what he reads upstairs in his room and what he reads downstairs around us," Mrs. Cilano added. When reading to himself, he is much slower compared to when reading to adults, and he pays more attention to the content, she said. Around adults he is inclined to show off and read material that is above his comprehension level, such as sections from the *New York Times*, added the mother.

CRACKING THE MYSTERY

Once John's reading behavior was chronologically tabulated and carefully examined, it was exciting to realize that much like in the earlier stories of Sean, Carrie, Brian, and Alicia, a clear pattern emerged in his reading development, one that had a distinct sequence of steps or stages of development. It appears that he, too, experienced a preliminary period of gaining general awareness of books and print, which started, in his case, during the first month of life. This included exposure to *Sesame Street* as his mother was nursing him. Somewhat later his parents started reading to him daily. He also played with block letters and enjoyed flipping the pages of books and magazines during that phase.

At twelve months, new reading behaviors became evident. John was able to name some of the letters and recognize several sign words. During the following months, his letter knowledge and sight vocabulary grew, simultaneously. And at fifteen months, "things really started to happen." He received a magnetic alphabet set, became obsessed with the letters, and his reading development started accelerating rapidly.

By sixteen months, Mr. Cilano thought it would be wise to encourage John's knowledge of the sounds of the letters, and the boy (probably with his parent's encouragement) focused his interest for awhile on the letters' sounds. Shortly thereafter, at eighteen months, John began to "make" simple words with his letters (which is a beginning form of writing), and putting together words became a central interest of his.

At twenty-four months, he started taking an active role in his parents' readings to him—first reading words, and shortly thereafter sentences, with which he was familiar. When he was about thirty-six months old and having gained some confidence, he slowly started to read by himself unfamiliar text, sounding out each difficult word. At forty-eight months, his reading became more fluent, and instead of reading for the mental challenge of the task he began to read for enjoyment of content.

This progression of reading behavior (which was natural like oral language acquisition, with activities evolving spontaneously and without planning) can be crystallized into a number of distinct steps or stages. As with the other children described in this book, an important reading concept or skill on which the boy had focused for a period of several months characterizes each of these stages. And while each stage appeared to be a prerequisite for the following stage, a necessary step in the process of reading acquisition, it is important to note that its distinctive reading behavior did not terminate when the new stage evolved. It continued to be present, as needed, but with less intensity and interest. It was as though the skill involved needed to be practiced, and mastered, while being of central interest to the child, and once this had been achieved, the child could move on.

THE STAGES IN JOHN'S READING DEVELOPMENT

Following is a summary of stages in John's reading development:

Stage 1: A preliminary period of gaining awareness of books and print (starting at one month).
Stage 2: Beginning to acquire letter knowledge and a sight vocabulary (starting at twelve months).

Stage 3: Beginning to learn the sounds of the letters (starting at sixteen months).

Stage 4: Beginning to put simple words together (eighteen months).

Stage 5: Participating in his parents' readings to him (twenty-four months).

Stage 6: Ability to read simple books by himself (thirty-six months).

Stage 7: Enjoying reading for content (forty-eight months).

THE PARENTS' ROLE IN JOHN'S READING DEVELOPMENT

What sparked the emergence of these stages? There is no doubt that the Cilanos placed a high value on good reading ability, and had a strong desire that John grow up to like books. Anticipating his arrival, they filled their home with children's books even before he was born. Moreover, while stating that they never intended to teach John to read, they did believe that parents should help youngsters in their reading attempts whenever their children show an interest—without making too much of a structured situation out of it. Thus, while appearing sincerely to believe that John had learned to read early because of an innate ability, with them only nurturing that ability, it appears from the information the Cilanos provided that they did spend a great deal of time with him—working, playing, and teaching, albeit all naturally, spontaneously, incidentally, and unsystematically. They encouraged John's reading development much like parents who encourage their child who learns to speak.

From the age of fifteen months until he was about forty months old, the Cilanos had print-related interactions with John on a daily basis. They read to him and with him, pointing at the words; they made rhymes with words in stories; they helped him learn the sounds of the letters and how to put together words; they encouraged him to sound out words; and they played many word, letter, and spelling games with him. They also provided John with a rich selection of reading toys and books, carefully matching these with his ability level.

It is important to emphasize that most of these print interactions were spontaneous and nonsystematic. Activities were usually embedded in John's routine daily activities. And the Cilanos were sensitive to stimulate and encourage him at his level of ability and understanding. They also worked hard (though sometimes failing) to make each print interaction a playful, enjoyable experience. And the process took on a life of its own, following an intrinsically natural sequence.

Chapter Eight

———

Bilingual Jenny

Around 1284, eyeglasses are invented in Venice or Florence, saving the reading lives of those with poor sight.
—Albert Manguel, *A History of Reading*

THE CHENG FAMILY

We will end our tour of natural readers' environments with a visit with the Chengs. Identified as a reader when she was four years old, Jenny is the only child portrayed in this book whose mother had planned, when pregnant, eventually to teach her child to read. And yet the Chengs, like the other parents described, had no systematic approach to this endeavor. Most of their print interactions with their child turned out to be intuitive, often spontaneous, following a naturally evolving sequence. It is interesting to observe the similarity between Jenny's sequence of reading development and the reading development of the children in the previous stories, who reportedly had learned to read early because of some unique innate ability.

Jenny's account is interesting for another reason. She was the only bilingual child in the study, a Chinese-speaking girl, who learned to read English at the same time she learned to speak the language—around age two. (Children usually speak their native language long before they learn to read it.) So, let us take a closer look at Jenny's reading development in English, beginning with a profile of the child, her parents, and their home environment.

Jenny's parents arrived from Taiwan three years before she was born to study economics at the local university. They were married in the United States and Jenny and her ten-month-old brother were born here. Mrs. Cheng, thirty, received her master's degree; Mr. Cheng, thirty-three, is now working on his doctoral dissertation. They live in a small student apartment near campus. Mr. Cheng has a graduate assistantship, while Mrs. Cheng is a full-time homemaker, busy raising their two young children. Her affluent parents, who live in Taiwan, help support this young family.

The family is Confucian, and they highly value education. "We are very educated people," Mrs. Cheng repeatedly remarked, and they would like to see Jenny become "very educated" as well. Deciding to speak Chinese at home, they refuse to give in to Jenny's periodic requests to speak more English with her. "She has to know her heritage," her mother explained, "and she will have to know how to speak in both languages."

Their culturally ingrained respect for education was the stated reason for Mrs. Cheng's desire to teach Jenny to read early. It was also the motivation behind their decision to remain in the United States at the end of their studies, they said. Critical of the Taiwanese school system for being nonstimulating and putting too much emphasis on trivial homework, the Chengs feel they can give Jenny much better schooling here. There is also less attention in Taiwan to gifted children, they explained.

As for early childhood education, Mrs. Cheng feels strongly that the early years are important for children's development, so important that she refuses to leave them with a sitter, even for short periods of time. "No one can replace my work with the children," she declares. Highly energetic and career oriented, she intends to develop it, but she plans to work only part time, and only after their younger child is in nursery school. "If a mother does not teach her child, she loses an important opportunity," she explained. And she firmly believes that had she worked outside the home and left Jenny with a sitter, the child would not have become an early reader. Interestingly, as proud as she is of Jenny's early ability, considering it to be a valuable asset, she maintains that most children could learn to read in their preschool years provided they receive the proper support from their parents. This is the common view among educated Asians, in particular of Chinese, Japanese, and Korean background, whether they live in the United States or abroad. The Chengs do not anticipate any problems to arise from Jenny's early ability, and they plan to teach also their younger son to read once he reaches the age of eighteen months.

JENNY

Let us take a closer look at Jenny. Tall, on the chubby side, with short smooth hair and large dark eyes, it was somewhat of a surprise to hear that she was a premature baby who spent her first seven days in an incubator. (She was born after a gestation period of seven and one-half months, weighing 5 lbs., 7 oz.) Once she was taken home, Jenny lost another pound, but then started gaining weight so rapidly that after three months she was placed on a diet. She has been big and tall ever since, Mrs. Cheng recounted. Her overall development was normal, except for a weak eye that required corrective surgery at age four. She also needs to wear glasses for reading, and she is not enthusiastic about it, her mother related.

Often reserved and shy around strangers—"so typically Chinese," Mrs. Cheng says—Jenny is a happy and cheerful child. She is also sensitive, curious, and somewhat withdrawn, and she has the same disposition as her father: "very bright but reserved," her mother explained. But she "is beginning to open up now," Mrs. Cheng reflected. She is not an easy child, though, reported her mother, having a strong personality and very strong feelings about people and things around her. Outwardly, she will obey her parents and never argue with them, but "she will show that she is uncomfortable." (The mother's remark should be taken in context of the Chinese culture that fosters strict obedience to adults from an early age.) Not seeking the company of children, Jenny interacts at this point primarily with her infant brother, with whom she reportedly loves to play, and with adults, in particular her mother. She seems to be a loner in nursery school. She will communicate with the teachers and participate in music and dancing activities, but will not interact much with the children. She prefers to entertain herself with books, puzzles, and artwork, Mrs. Cheng recounted.

Our attempts to measure Jenny's intelligence on the Peabody Picture Vocabulary Test at age four years, one month were unsuccessful. The tester thought the results were unfair because she was more fluent in Chinese than in English. The Stanford Binet Intelligence Scale also provided an inappropriate measure of her true mental abilities because of her relative limited English fluency, explained the tester. And so we were left guessing.

And what does Jenny like to do? How does she spend her days? Reading used to be her favorite activity until she was four years, four months old, Mrs. Cheng related. Then she started taking violin lessons by the Suzuki method, and she has been enjoying that so much that she now prefers playing the violin to reading, said Mrs. Cheng. Both mother and daughter love the shared practice sessions, giving it two full hours a day, she says, which they divide into four, thirty-minute segments. Jenny also likes to do puzzles—sometimes for as long as an hour at a time—she listens to recorded music, builds Lego houses and castles, and draws and paints. But, overall, "she is not a very toy-oriented child," Mrs. Cheng reflected, and has never been interested in dolls, for example, she said.

HOW WELL COULD SHE READ?

Choosing to have all of our interviews on campus, Mrs. Cheng brought Jenny to one of the sessions for her reading assessment. It was the end of a morning in nursery school and Jenny appeared somewhat tired. Still, she read the six criterion sentences fluently, making only one slight error, reading *It's raining* instead of *It is raining*.

She then read fluently, with no mistakes, the title and seven sentences from "The Happy Woman," a story in the primer. She read fluently with no mistake the title and nine sentences from "Little Blue and Little Yellow" in the first-grade reader.

She seemed to get involved with that story and began to ask questions. Reluctant to be moved to the next story, she casually picked up a third-grade reader lying on my desk, but when I asked her to read from it, she refused. She lost interest, and would read no further, reaching out instead for a stack of blocks at the corner of my desk. I decided to stop the assessment at that point.

Mrs. Cheng felt uncomfortable about Jenny's reluctance to cooperate, blaming the text's small print, and the fact that Jenny's pediatrician had discouraged her from reading small print because of a congenital eye problem. And she kept maintaining that Jenny could technically read "from any book, including her father's textbooks in economy." Whenever she comes to a difficult word, she sounds it out, Mrs. Cheng explained. And when she reads a word she does not understand, she will ask for a translation. But she obviously does not understand everything that she is reading, having only a four-year-old's mind, Mrs. Cheng added.

HOW DID SHE LEARN TO READ?

So how did a Chinese-speaking child acquire, by age four, the ability to read English on at least a first-grade level? And, admitting that she had encouraged Jenny's reading development, what exactly did Mrs. Cheng do? As it turned out, until Jenny was eighteen months old, there was little difference between her mother and other mothers in respect to literacy development. Although she had always intended to teach Jenny to read, Mrs. Cheng did not follow any formal instructional methodology. But it came across clearly in the interviews that she approached the matter with a quiet determination to achieve her goal, and with no doubt in her mind that Jenny could do it. She approached reading the same way she approached all other aspects of the child's development: naturally, intuitively, with patience, persistence, and great sensitivity. So how did Jenny learn to read? To fully understand her literacy development, the fine interplay between her and her parents, let us once again follow the chronicle of a natural reader's development.

Pulling Books Off the Shelves

When Jenny was about one year old, her favorite activity was to pull her parents' books off the shelves. She liked to turn the pages and pretend to read from them, Mrs. Cheng recalled. She "read" in baby talk, and no one could understand what she was saying, but she kept doing that for a period of several months. Nothing else in Jenny's reading behavior impressed her parents as particularly noteworthy at that period, Mrs. Cheng recounted.

When she was about eighteen months old, several events occurred that would in time affect her literacy development. To begin with, the Chengs decided to give Jenny some preschool experience to help her become more sociable. And they enrolled her in a Chinese Sunday school that met for an hour and a half every week. She received some religious instruction, learned a few Bible stories, and sang Chinese songs, they say.

During that period, Jenny also started to watch *Sesame Street*, but after getting a daily one-hour dose of the program, for about a month, she started complaining that *Sesame Street* was repetitive, and she lost interest, recounted Mrs. Cheng. But this program was instrumental in helping her establish her letter knowledge, acknowledged the mother. Since then, Jenny would watch *Sesame Street* only sporadically, being "one of those rare children who do not like to watch television," said Mrs. Cheng. And whenever she would suggest to the child to go watch some television (so that she could have some time for herself), Jenny would respond with a countersuggestion such as taking a walk, going to the library, or doing some reading together. She preferred any of these activities to television, explained Mrs. Cheng.

Becoming Bilingual

But the most important event, by eighteen months, was the Chengs decision to start teaching Jenny English. They were very proud of their Chinese heritage, and would continue to instill that heritage in Jenny, but it was also important that she learn to speak and read the local language, they said. And there was no doubt in their mind that their child could do that, and moreover, that it was their responsibility to help her achieve that goal— with the right activities and for the appropriate length of time.

Using English picture books as an aid, Mrs. Cheng started reading to Jenny from these books, translating the words to Chinese. She read to her daily, pointing at the words, discussing the pictures, and Jenny slowly began to acquire an English vocabulary while at the same time learning to recognize these words in print. To facilitate the child's learning, Mrs. Cheng also started to coach Jenny with the letters, recalling how she herself was taught English, starting with the letters.

She then prepared small cards, marking each with a capital letter, and both parents started playing a variety of simple letter games with Jenny. They would hold up a letter and ask her "What's that?" or, giving her the name of a letter, they would ask her to find it in the stack of cards, and so on. It was a play activity, Mrs. Cheng explained, and it stimulated Jenny mentally. They also gave her a set of wooden alphabet blocks, and Mrs. Cheng made cardboard letter blocks from a pattern she had found on a cereal box. Jenny loved to play with these blocks— with the homemade blocks even more than with the commercial ones—the mother recalled. Within about a month, the child learned to recognize and name all uppercase letters, Mrs. Cheng related. They were so impressed by her ability that they started to teach Jenny the numbers from one to ten, she added.

Taking Trips to the Public Library

Shortly thereafter, Jenny started taking weekly trips to the public library. Mrs. Cheng, reportedly an avid reader who makes extensive use of the library, started taking Jenny along with her, checking out several books for her at each visit. And the public library became the main source of reading material for this early reader. Strapped for space in their small apartment, which was crammed with their own schoolbooks, the Chengs decided not to buy books for Jenny but use the library instead. They started checking out counting picture books and ABC books that had a few words per page, reading to her daily from these books.

By the time she was twenty-one months, Jenny knew the names of all the lowercase letters in addition to the uppercase letters, her mother recalled, and she would often entertain herself matching the uppercase with the lowercase letters. Her memory was so good that she could memorize a new book after only one reading, her mother said. And increasingly she would recognize familiar words in new reading material. But her English comprehension was still limited, Mrs. Cheng explained, and Jenny would often come to her asking for the meaning of a particular word she did not understand. "What does C-A-T mean?" Jenny would ask, for example, or "What does C-A-R mean?" identifying the word by its spelling. Mr. Cheng summed up that period between age one and a half and two as the time when Jenny "tried to remember the letters and also the words." Or, to put it in other words, she learned to speak English and to read English at the same time. (As mentioned earlier, this is not the usual course of events with one's native language. Children usually have a good speaking vocabulary before they start learning to read, though some linguists propose that in the contemporary literate environment, children can learn to read simultaneously with learning to speak that language.)

By the time Jenny was two, easy picture books did not satisfy her anymore and she started to ask for books with "more words than pictures," Mrs. Cheng recalled. So, for Christmas, the Chengs gave her the fifteen-volume set of *Child Craft Encyclopedia*, published by the World Book Company—among the few books they did agree to buy for her. At first, Jenny showed interest only in the first two volumes, *Nursery Poems and Rhymes* and *Short Stories and Fables*, and the Chengs would read to her daily from these volumes. To maximize this learning opportunity, they decided also to check out library records with the same rhymes, and Jenny would often listen to the records while pretending to read the rhymes in her encyclopedia. At first she "could read only a few words," but the mother made a point of encouraging Jenny's reading and build up her confidence. "I would read some, and Jenny would read some," she explained. Then they started alternating their reading, taking turns sentence by sentence, then page by page. "It was like a game," explained the mother, and slowly Jenny would memorize the complete rhymes.

Reading with Jenny

From age two until Jenny started to enjoy reading by herself (around age three), Mrs. Cheng would read with her every evening for about an hour, she said. Also Mr. Cheng would try to read with her every day, but he could give it only "a little time." Continuously eager to facilitate her child's reading development, Mrs. Cheng searched for additional fun activities to stimulate the child's learning. And when she heard of a series of workshops for Chinese parents, given by a Chinese university graduate who ran a nursery school in her home, Mrs. Cheng decided to join. Demonstrating to parents didactic games they could make themselves to use with their children to promote beginning reading and math skills, she incorporated many of these games in her print interactions with Jenny. Following is a sample of these activities as reported by her mother:

Word-and-Picture Lotto. The child is given a sheet of cardboard with several words printed on it. Small cards with matching pictures are added. The objective of the game is to match the pictures with the corresponding words. Some of the words that Mrs. Cheng used with Jenny included *Mitten, Thumb, Bird, Books, Jet, Onion, Lamb, House, Fish,* and *Rabbit.*

Card Matching. The child is given an assortment of cards showing pictures of objects. Each picture has two corresponding cards, one in English and one in Chinese. The objective of the game is to match the English words with the Chinese words and place them on the corresponding picture. Some of the words that Mrs. Cheng used in that game included *Donkey, Drink, Telephone, Stop,* and *Turtle.*

Puppets and Rhymes. The child is presented with a set of figures cut out of cardboard. Characteristic features of these figures are drawn on one side with a matching action rhyme printed on the back. The objective of the game is to manipulate a figure while reading (or reciting) the corresponding rhyme. At first, Mrs. Cheng used to read the rhymes and Jenny would repeat them. After several months, Jenny was able to recite the rhymes by herself as she was manipulating the figures. One of her favorite set of figures was of the Five Little Snowmen, recalled Mrs. Cheng. She loved to play with those figures reciting the following rhymes:

Five little snowmen
outside my door;
one melts away,
then there are four.

Four little snowmen
playing with me;
one melts away,
then there are three.

Three little snowmen
playing with you;
one melts away,
then there were two.

Two little snowmen
eating a bun;
one melts away,
then there is one.

One little snowman
standing alone;
one melts away,
then all the snowmen are gone.

Flower Words. The child is given a flower cut out of cardboard, with a revolving center that has a closing syllable printed on it. Different letters are marked on each petal. As the center is turned and the closing syllable gets aligned with one lettered petal after another, words are formed. Mrs. Cheng made many such flower words for Jenny. One of Jenny's favorites, she recalled, featured the letters *S*, *B*, *R*, and *K* on the petals, with the closing syllable *ING* at the center. She could then form words such as *S-ing*, *B-ing*, *R-ing*, and *K-ing*.

Rhyming Words. The child is presented with a list of unfamiliar words that have the same ending syllable. Once she knows that syllable, she has to sound out only the first letter of each word to be able to read the whole list. For example, if the ending syllable was *IGHT*, words on Jenny's list included *T-ight*,

R-ight, *N-ight*, *L-ight*, *F-ight*, and later on *Fr-ight*, *Pl-ight*, *Br-ight*. Another list had *AIL* as its ending syllable, with words such as *S-ail*, *N-ail*, *R-ail*, *F-ail*, and then *Sn-ail*, *Tr-ail*, and so forth. These word lists helped Jenny "learn to go on reading even if she did not understand the meaning of what she was reading," explained Mrs. Cheng.

The beauty of these homemade games is their individualized nature. Each child, at each step of development, can be given different words to fit his or her interests. Between ages two and two and a half, Jenny's mother played these games with her often two or three times a week, she said. Later on, Jenny would play these games by herself. "It was like a toy for her," remarked Mrs. Cheng, and it improved her reading.

When she was two years, seven months old, Jenny started to attend the campus nursery school, three mornings a week, in addition to her Chinese Sunday school. The Chengs hoped that this program would improve her English as well as her social skills. But Jenny had a hard time adjusting to the place, according to Mrs. Cheng. She cried a lot and kept complaining that she could not understand what the children were saying. Still, her English vocabulary improved at a faster rate, and she was soon able to pick up an unfamiliar book and identify "many" of its words, recounted Mrs. Cheng.

An Interest in Spelling

Her fascination with words then led to an interest in spelling, and she began to spend time making words with her letter blocks. "She always wanted to know how to spell a word," her mother commented, often asking how to spell this or that word. "How do you spell *Dog*?" she would ask, for example, saying the word in Chinese, or, "Mommy, spell *Cat* for me." And Mrs. Cheng would name the English letters of that word, with Jenny putting the word together with her letter blocks.

When Mrs. Cheng became pregnant with her second child, there were some problems and she had to be especially careful and rest a lot to prevent another premature birth. And so, from age two and a half until Jenny's brother was born, she reduced her work time with Jenny. "There was a decline in her reading ability during that period," Mr. Cheng remarked. Mrs. Cheng had a somewhat different view, saying, "Jenny continued to make progress all along, on her own, because of the good foundation she had received."

In any case, by age three Jenny had the technical ability to read from any text, recounted Mrs. Cheng, including her father's textbooks. But the mother continued to choose her reading material carefully, to match the text's difficulty with the child's level of comprehension. This was important, she said, to "build Jenny's sense of success in her reading."

Culturally driven to develop the child's mental ability, as much as she could, once Jenny was able to read English, her parents enrolled her in another Chinese school that met one afternoon a week for two hours. The objective of that school was to develop the Chinese literacy skills of children of Chinese background. And so, at age three, Jenny was attending three different programs. In each of these settings, she preferred quiet, solitary activities over active interactions with children, her mother related. She was adult-oriented, and much like her father, "she likes to obey the teachers very much," Mrs. Chengadded.

To top all this activity, when Jenny was about four years old, her mother started visiting the university's Reading Center to check out second- and third-grade-level books for her. This was Jenny's actual reading level at the time, and the mother looked for books with a higher-than-usual ratio of pictures per text and as such more appealing to preschoolers. While Jenny was often more interested in the easier primers, her mother would select the more difficult books "because she does not know what her level is and these books are more appropriate for her level," she explained.

Reading Bedtime Stories to her Father

With all this adult attention, is it any surprise that Jenny's reading fluency continuously improved? By the time of the interviews, when she was four years, five months old, she was reading a bedtime story to her father, every night, as he was putting her to bed, recounted her mother.

CRACKING THE PUZZLE

So what was the secret of Jenny's reading development, if one can still consider it a secret? Why did she learn to read early when so many other children of similar age do not? Furthermore, what was the process of her reading development, and how does it compare with the reading development of Sean, Carrie, Brian, Alicia, and John? No one could deny that Mrs. Cheng's determination to teach Jenny, and her calm confidence in the child's ability to master reading early, had provided the impetus for Jenny's learning. That determination distinguishes this story from the other children's—except perhaps for Alicia's, whose mother had also been quite determined to develop her reading from an early age.

It is also clear that the Chengs' attitude reflects the family's Confucian background, with its strong emphasis on education. As mentioned earlier, early learning and parents' support of it is highly valued among most educated Asian parents. And children of Chinese background, in the United States as well as in Asia, are encouraged to learn to read early. Mrs. Cheng was just as confident that without her support Jenny would not have become an early reader.

It is interesting, therefore, that in spite of this culturally ingrained attitude toward early learning, the Chengs' style of work/play with Jenny was fundamentally not different from that of the other parents described. Also they had no systematic strategy to achieve that goal, approaching the matter more or less intuitively: stimulating, encouraging, coaching, supporting, while all along sensitively basing their print interactions with Jenny on her interests and level of ability. Learning situations—except for those adopted from the special workshop—often occurred incidentally, quite naturally. And the specifics of these interactions were surprisingly, basically, similar to the interactions found in the homes of the other five children: helping Jenny learn the names of the letters and acquire a sight vocabulary; reading daily to her, often pointing at the words; patiently assisting her in her spelling efforts; and, most importantly, playing a variety of letter-sound and word games with her.

A careful analysis of the chronology of Jenny's reading behavior reveals an emerging developmental process, one that had an intrinsic sequence. And this sequence was very similar to that of the other children described.

THE STAGES IN JENNY'S READING DEVELOPMENT

For Jenny, as with the other children, there was first a preliminary period in which she gained awareness and some general knowledge about books and print. While we have little information about that period, we know that at twelve months, she enjoyed playing with her parents' books, turning pages, and pretending to read in baby talk. Overall, she was trying to imitate her parents' outward reading behavior, they said.

The age of eighteen months marked a milestone. Mrs. Cheng started teaching Jenny to speak and read English, using picture books to aid her. And although it was the child's second language, she acquired, very much like Sean, Carrie, Brian, Alicia, and John, letter knowledge and sight vocabulary simultaneously.

Some six months later, at the age of twenty-four months, Jenny made a conceptual leap when she began to take an active role in her mother's readings to her: "reading" the words she could recognize. And as Mrs. Cheng was playing the different reading games with her, Jenny's participation became increasingly more substantial.

Again, following another six-month period, by the time she was about thirty months old, Jenny took another step forward. She was now "reading" by herself familiar nursery rhymes. And she also started to show an interest in spelling, often trying to form words with her letter blocks.

At thirty-six months, Jenny reached the technical ability to read easy, unfamiliar books. Her comprehension level was still limited, but gradually, as her vocabulary improved, her enjoyment in reading increased. At forty-eight months, she was reading unfamiliar bedtime stories to her father.

This sequence of development, basically so similar to the reading development of Sean, Carrie, Brian, Alicia, and John, suggests again the existence of steps or stages in the process of natural reading development. Natural, because learning situations evolved intuitively, often spontaneously, and were not based on any systematic method of instruction. And each step, marked by a distinctive reading behavior, appears to be a pre-requisite for the following step, a necessary rung in the child's developmental process. These steps or stages for Jenny can be summarized as follows:

Stage 1: A preliminary period of gaining general awareness of books and print (ongoing at twelve months).

Stage 2: Acquiring letter knowledge and a sight vocabulary (beginning at eighteen months).

Stage 3: Participating in mother's readings to her (starting at twenty-four months).

Stage 4: Learning the sounds of letters (beginning at twenty-four months).

Stage 5: Forming words with letter blocks (starting at thirty months).

Stage 6: Technical ability to read easy, unfamiliar text (from thirty-six months).

Stage 7: Reading for enjoyment of content (from forty-eight months).

It is important to emphasize that Mrs. Cheng got much satisfaction out of Jenny's early reading ability. And while she considers herself to be an active and career-oriented woman, she feels that her time at home with Jenny was well spent and worthwhile.

Part III

Learning to Read Naturally

Chapter Nine

Natural Reading Development

Every time a child climbs on someone's lap to hear a
story, literacy learning takes place. Every time a child
tells someone what to write on a blank piece of paper
and watches her words become print, she learns about
the power of language.
— N. Lynne Decker Collins and Margaret B. Shaeffer,
"Look, Listen, and Learn to Read"

A DEVELOPMENTAL PROCESS IN STAGES

The preceding chapters provide a detailed account of six early
readers and their experience with literacy: six children who
came from different family backgrounds, whose parents had
never met, and who had no systematic instruction, yet they
learned to read in their preschool years. Once the reading development of these children was chronologically tabulated and
carefully compared, it was exciting to realize that although their
learning was informal and unstructured, they all experienced a
surprisingly similar process of reading development, one that incorporated several distinct stages.

Each of these stages (or phases), lasting several months, appears to be a prerequisite for the following stage, a necessary rung

in the children's ladder of reading development. And in each stage, the children's reading-related knowledge grew more comprehensive, slowly increasing their mastery of reading. (A full analysis of these stages can be found in an article I wrote in 1986.[1])

Looking at this process of development from a distance, one can picture the children engaged in a variety of literacy-related activities throughout their daily routine: interacting with picture books and encountering environmental print—on food labels, direction words, store names, coupons, advertisements in newspapers and magazines, restaurant menus, television, and so on. We can see them busy acting out a favorite story or real-life situations, incorporating elements of literacy, such as writing a letter to Grandma, helping mother prepare a shopping list, trying to read the instructions on a new toy, or playing a variety of word-and-letter games with their parents. All these reading- and writing-related activities would spontaneously appear and disappear throughout the daily repertoire of the children's behavior.

Yet within this busy, seemingly chaotic, realm of reading-related activities, one can discern the progressive line of concept and skill development of these children advancing from one stage to the next. As they engaged in the varied activities, each child at each stage of development was especially (but not exclusively) interested in one type of activity, which was based on one particular reading concept or skill, and focused on it for a period of several months. It was as if this desire to play/work (or be obsessive, as one parent remarked) with a particular reading concept or skill for a period of several months enabled that child to practice the knowledge that was involved, learn it, master it, and then move on.

Following is a combined summary of stages in the reading development of these children:

Stage 1: A preliminary period of gaining awareness and general knowledge about books and print (starting any time during the first year).

Stage 2: Learning the names of the letters and acquiring a beginning sight vocabulary (starting between twelve and eighteen months).

Stage 3: Learning the sounds of the letters (starting between twenty and twenty-four months).

Stage 4: Putting words together (starting between twenty-four and thirty-two months).

Stage 5: Reading aloud from familiar books (starting between twenty and thirty months).

Stage 6: Sounding out short, unfamiliar words (starting around thirty-two to thirty-four months).

Stage 7: Independent reading of easy, unfamiliar books (around thirty-six months).

Stage 8: Reading for enjoyment of content (around forty-eight months).

WHAT STIMULATES THIS PROCESS?

How did it happen? Without systematic instruction, how could children at that tender age experience basically the same developmental stages, achieving by age four an independent reading capability? My interviews with the parents revealed that they were instrumental in the children's reading development. These youngsters did not learn to read by themselves, as their parents have claimed or as popular belief often holds. Neither did these children possess an unusual innate ability for early reading that could have facilitated theirs (over other children's) early achievement.

It soon became apparent that while not planning to teach the children to read (except in one case), these parents did lend their strong support to the emerging learning process, sensitively following their youngsters' literacy questions and interests, and enthusiastically responding to these. Placing high value on good reading ability, these parents freely engaged their children in a variety of literacy activities. They were spontaneous and intuitive. And they had the patience and desire to stimulate and encourage each small step of progress. Most important perhaps, they tried to make each reading interaction an enjoyable, fun-filled experience.

What specifically did they do? Using a variety of techniques, we saw how they helped the children learn the names of the letters and their sounds. "Show me an *A*, show me a *B*," or "Which letter would you change that could make a new word?" were common games they played with their children. They coached them with a growing sight vocabulary—playfully, spontaneously—using street signs, storefront names, direction words, coupons, captions in magazines, and so forth, as teaching aids. "Where are we now, Carrie?" one couple would ask their child, then pointing at the store name, they'd give her the answer. All the parents helped their children with their spelling attempts, encouraging any effort they made to "make words" (often having great fun with rhymes, as for instance, "What rhymes with Mommy?" one mother would repeatedly start asking, with her son's favorite answer being "salami"). They all read books to and with their children every day, pointing at the words, and they would listen to the children read aloud to them—sometimes engaging in alternate reading.

This profusion of reading-related interactions was supported by a rich selection of reading and writing materials: from a large assortment of picture books and children's magazines and dictionaries to magnetic letters, block letters, word-and-letter flash cards, blackboard and chalk, crayons, pencils, markers, puzzles with words, workbooks, records of nursery rhymes and stories, and many other reading-related toys, which the parents and other family members continuously supplied. There was also an extensive use of educational television programs, *Sesame Street* in particular.

It is important to emphasize that, in addition to their active support of the ongoing learning process, all of these parents had an intuitive understanding of the importance of matching the degree of difficulty of a particular reading-related material or activity with the child's level of ability at the time. Careful to provide the maximum amount of successful reading experiences, they understood intuitively that unpleasant experiences could lead the children to frustration, setbacks, or even withdrawal from the reading experience. And they tried their best to avoid that. We see how without knowing, the activities these parents and children engaged in were developmentally appropriate.

So how could these parents honestly claim that their children had learned to read by themselves because of an innate ability for early reading? Well, it appears that they were partly right and partly wrong. They were wrong in claiming that the children had learned to read by themselves. Certainly, they did not. But because they had no initial intention to teach the children to read, and their help was spontaneous and unsystematic, these parents never considered their print interactions with the children to be a case of "teaching." They regarded these interactions to be a form of play, somewhat similar to parental vocalizations with an infant or toddler who learns to speak. Most parents also do not realize that they are their children's speech teachers—believing that cooing, babbling, and the usual baby talk they engage in with their infants and toddlers are just "cute" enjoyable interactions, and that children learn to talk because "it is in their genes." But we now know, from observations of children raised in European orphanages and from other studies, that when babies and toddlers are not being talked to, they do not learn to talk. We now know that even oral language development, not just written language development, is dependent on stimulation and support from the environment.[2] However, the parents were right in claiming that the children had an innate ability for reading. This point will be discussed later in this chapter.

But many preschoolers, you will say, have a variety of literacy-related interactions with their parents and still they do not become capable early readers. So why have the children portrayed in this book achieved independent reading capability in this informal manner? It appears that while apparently possessing no unusual personal qualities that could explain their achievement, their home environment did possess a number of factors that encouraged early reading development.

THE EMOTIONAL TRIGGER

To begin with, it soon became clear that these parents enjoyed long interactions with their children, and for one reason or another their interactions often centered around reading-related activities. They enjoyed these activities so much, from an early age, almost to the point of indulgence.

Moreover, these parents never felt bound by expert opinion or anyone else's for that matter, as to what they could or should do with their children—literacy wise—or what they should not do. They followed their own intuition. They felt they knew their children better than anyone else, and what was good for them. Once they thought their children were ready to acquire some reading-related knowledge, they went ahead, never hesitating to encourage that development, to stimulate it, and slowly they helped bring their children to the level of independent reading proficiency. Furthermore, they never believed they ought to postpone that development and wait for formal schooling. True, they did worry occasionally that they may be doing something wrong, which possibly could cause some future problem in school. But their desire to stimulate and develop their children was evidently stronger than some vague concerns about possible negative effects in the future.

Next, with the exception of the Taiwanese family, each of these families' reading activities had, at first, a different purpose than encouraging reading development. Each family was in a unique situation that created a conducive climate for reading-related interactions with their children. These special conditions may explain why these children became early readers when most preschoolers do not.

Let us take a closer look at our six children. In the case of Sean, we saw that his reading development became something of a hobby for his parents. Deriving much satisfaction from observing how much he developed, they approached reading-related activities as a family game. Why did they enjoy stimulating their child's early ability? Perhaps, in part, to compensate for their own frustrated educational ambition. Having completed his formal education with high school, the father may have derived special satisfaction from seeing his son become academically well developed. "Where did he get it from?" the Gallens kept asking each other. And their sense of amazement probably further encouraged their work and play with Sean around print-related activities. And so the process kept rolling, fueled by the child's natural curiosity to learn, and his parents' pleasure in encouraging that development.

In Carrie's case, it seems that reading activities provided the lifeline between that sensitive and restless child and her very busy parents. Burdened by the mother's sense of guilt for leaving the child with a babysitter all day long, with Carrie desperately craving their attention whenever they were home, the Millers found reading-related activities to be a mutually enjoyable medium between them. Moreover, they soon realized that these activities could be used anytime, day or night, always having the desired soothing effect on Carrie. From day one, the parents' reading voice became Carrie's lullaby, and print-related activities became the bond between this child and her parents.

In Brian's home, print-related activities were first engaged in as a means to keep him physically calm—a requirement imposed on the parents by the child's pediatrician due to Brian's asthmatic condition. It was during the long bedridden recuperation period, following Brian's first hospitalization, that the Giovannis began to provide him with intense reading-related activities. This was easy to do. It kept Brian busy and entertained, it did not cost much, and it developed the child's mental faculties. Stimulating the child's interest, these reading experiences led to a chain of action and reaction between parents and child that eventually culminated in an early reading capability.

As for Alicia, her mother was a professional teacher (used to thinking in terms of child development), so it should not be surprising that she felt challenged to find out what could actually be done about infants' and toddlers' mental development. She even felt it was her responsibility to try to develop her daughter's reading ability. But there was an additional motivation in the Gibson home to encourage Alicia's early development. An early reading ability, assumed to facilitate higher mental capability, justified in her parents' minds the mother's resignation from her teaching career—a serious financial sacrifice in their case. It made the mother's decision to be a stay-at-home mom more worthwhile and rewarding for them.

John's home had an air of anxiety about it, which may have found some outlet in his parents' heightened concern for his development. The father was concerned that John would become a poor reader like his cousin unless he, personally, did something about it. The mother was worried that John would follow in her sister's footsteps and not realize his potential, unless they actively did something to develop his talent. So the Cilanos started to focus on reading-related activities from an early age, to reassure themselves that the experience of other family members would not be repeated.

Jenny is the only child in our group of early readers whose mother had planned, already when pregnant, eventually to teach her child to read. This decision was grounded in her Confucian background. But even Mrs. Cheng had a broader motive in mind: like most educated Chinese (and without the latest information from brain-development research), she intuitively considered early reading development to be a good means of developing the child's overall mental capability.

In each of our young readers' homes, we see a strong motivation to focus on reading activities beyond the simple desire to stimulate the children's development. This pervading motivation could explain why these children became capable early readers without formal systematic instruction, when most children do not. Their homes were more sensitive and attentive to print, and more lavish with print-related activities, compared with the home environments of most preschoolers. Moreover, as the children's ability progressed, their reading development became something of an adventure for their families, a mental game—to see how far the children could develop. From the parents' points of view, as long as the children enjoyed the activities, there could be no harm in them. And they concluded that since their children would have to learn to read anyhow, why not start to encourage that learning process as soon as the children were ready.

FROM THE FEW TO THE MANY

Can the story of reading development of our six children teach something to the general population of children? Is this a representative sample? Times have changed. The nation's attitude toward early reading development has changed. Following three decades of research on early reading development, combined with insight from brain research, the National Association for the Education of Young Children (NAEYC) together with the International Reading Association (IRA) came out, in 1998, with a joint position statement. In this statement, titled *Learning to Read and Write: Developmentally Appropriate Practices for Young Children*, the two organizations recognize the critical importance of the early years for the development of literacy and children's higher standard of achievements: "Failing to give children literacy experiences until they are school age can severely limit the reading and writing levels they ultimately attain."[3] These two national organizations have now adopted a similar attitude toward early literacy development as the parents of natural early readers have held for years.

Although one cannot talk in absolute terms on the basis of a small sample, one cannot ignore the striking similarities that were found in these independent cases. The fact that six preschool children from different family backgrounds, with varying levels of IQ, have learned to read with no systematic instruction, yet experiencing such a similar, sequentially logic process of development, is significant. A similarity such as this cannot be coincidental. It may indicate the existence of a general pattern of mental development that may apply to most, if not all, preschoolers and their parents.

This similarity may suggest that a natural, innate process of reading development may start and slowly unfold among preschoolers who live in a responsively literate and supportive home environment. "Research also indicates that emerging literacy skills begin to develop in infancy, . . . there appears to be a sensitive period in which such skills develop more easily, and evidence points to a genetic/environment interaction that promotes such development," write Doris Bergen and Juliet Coscia in *Brain Research and Childhood Education*.[4] By "responsively literate" I mean that, in addition to the rich selection of books and print-related materials—available today in many youngsters' homes—parents have an active attitude toward their children's literacy development. Finely tuned to their children's reading and writing interests, these parents enjoy encouraging and stimulating that development.

NATURAL READING DEVELOPMENT

By "a natural process" I mean that this process of development is neither directed nor guided by the parents or some standard reading-instruction methodology, with the adult having the active role and the child being passive. The natural process unfolds within each child as a result of the interaction between him or her and a responsive environment. The sequence, the order of development within this process of reading acquisition, is intrinsically regulated. The timing may vary from one child to another, but no adult can change that order; very much like in the case of children learning to talk, who first experience a babbling period, then a one-word period, followed by a two-word period, and so forth, with no adult having the power to change that sequence. In a natural process of reading development, children will absorb from their encounters with print only what fits their stage on the ladder of reading development. Parents (or other significant adults) can provide necessary stimulation, feedback, and support, but they cannot dictate the order of development.

The informal flavor of natural reading acquisition was beautifully captured by William Teale who wrote:

> Becoming literate before schooling does occur for the vast majority of early readers-writers in the course of normal daily interactions in the home and community and with no formal instructions. The process, however, can profitably be described as involving both learning (on the part of the child) and teaching (on the part of the parent[s] or other significant literate persons in the child's environment). However, the teaching that occurs in homes looks nothing like what is typically thought of as teaching in classrooms. Yes, there is some of what may be termed "direct instruction": "This is a D," "That says fish," teaching children to name the letters of the alphabet. But most of the teaching occurs as an aspect of the social interaction between parent and child in activities typical of the home or community which are mediated by literacy. . . . Both social context and internal properties of the child mediate the acquisition of literacy. Any story of how children learn to read and write (naturally) must reflect the fact that social interaction and cognition are intimately bound.[5]

Some may argue that the parents' drive is more important than the child's initiative in the process of early reading acquisition. This reminds one of the chicken-and-the-egg question. We know that children have a natural curiosity to learn about their environment, and literacy is an integral part of today's environment. But children also need encouragement and support in their learning efforts, to be given in the right amount and at the right time. Again, comparing reading development with speech development, we know that children have the built-in capacity to learn to talk, yet they need an adult to vocally communicate with them from early infancy, for many months and through different phases of linguistic development, before they can talk on their own. Without early adult communication, children will not learn to talk. The same is true of early reading development.

Research findings from the 1960s and 1970s extensively indicate that preschool children have the capacity to learn how to read.[6] Studies from the 1980s and 1990s show that most American children begin their reading and writing development in their preschool years.[7] The children portrayed in this book demonstrate how natural early reading capability is acquired when parents provide the continuous necessary stimulation, feedback, and support. There is all the reason to believe that given similar conditions, most preschoolers could achieve similar results.

NATURAL READING DEVELOPMENT AND CHILDREN IN POVERTY

So let us assume that most preschoolers who will be immersed in a responsively literate environment, at home and/or in a good preschool program, will experience natural reading development. But what about children living in poverty, or in non-English-speaking and/or culturally diverse families? Could these children learn to read English naturally? This question is of special concern to teachers because of the disparity in the achievements of children from low- and middle-income families.

It is important to keep in mind that natural reading development is not stimulated by a bank account, but by an attitude. Many poor children are as capable or incapable of learning to read as affluent children are, and many poor parents care just as much about their children's development as affluent parents do. Furthermore, many poor families have capable members who could be encouraged and guided, if needed—by teachers, community centers, parents' programs, family literacy programs, and so on—to stimulate their children's natural reading development. "Studies suggest that blanket assertions that poor homes are characterized by a disregard for the value of literacy and an absence of literacy practices are overgeneralizations that blatantly ignore research evidence," writes Elsa Auerbach.[8] Poor families may often lack the confidence in their knowledge and ability to help their children, but this confidence can be developed with proper guidance. "Parent–teacher partnerships will have the potential to make a difference in helping poor, linguistically and culturally different children experience greater success in American schools," according to Jeanne Paratore, Gigliana Melzi, and Barbara Krol-Sinclair.[9]

There is a philosophical issue here, brought up already by Carl Bereiter, the cofounder of a successful preschool program developed in the 1960s to help disadvantaged children. In a scathing monograph titled *Must We Educate?* Bereiter examined the notion that there are basically two possible explanations for the lower achievements of poor children: the "deficit" explanation and the "difference" explanation. "The deficit explanation holds that poor children, because of environmental conditions and possibly because of heredity, are lacking in some of the traits necessary for successful school learning. The difference explanation holds that poor children . . . are not deficient in any basic way but have cultural differences that are not appreciated by the schools."[10] This philosophical and politically charged question is still relevant today. And there is no consensus about it. Poor and marginalized communities in the United States are free to choose their explanation; but it is important to keep in mind that the explanation they choose will determine the community's educational attitude and practice. More insight into this topic can be found in *Many Families, Many Literacies* by Denny Taylor.[11]

Basically, I agree with Taylor's positive statement: "Families are the primary literacy resource for their children—racial and ethnic identity should not be used explicitly or implicitly to suggest that families live in households that lack social and intellectual resources."[12] Having coined the concept of family literacy, Taylor speaks out against the deficit-driven attitude toward poor and marginalized families. I also support Susan B. Neuman's recommendation: "The best way to meet the challenge of educating children from various cultural backgrounds is to provide them with the very best quality of instruction, which includes high standards, direct instruction, time, materials, and opportunities for activities that encourage children's self-discovery and explorations. Such programs are likely to benefit all children from all cultural and economic groups to become competent members of the larger community of readers and writers."[13] But to do this effectively, communities will have to provide needy parents with encouragement and guidance on how to create a responsively literate home environment. Much work along this line has already been started.[14]

NATURAL READING DEVELOPMENT AND NON-ENGLISH-SPEAKING FAMILIES

Some will claim that non-English-speaking families could not support the natural reading development of their youngsters. Chapter 8 recounts the story of a native Chinese-speaking preschooler who learned to read English naturally, as a second language, at the same time that she learned to speak English. In Jenny Cheng's cultural and family background, the need to learn a second language was viewed as an advantage rather than a disadvantage; a gain rather than a deficit.

In my own family, I had the opportunity to observe our younger son, three-year-old Ariel, learn to read English, naturally, as a second language. He learned to function both in Hebrew and English, one language spoken at home, the other outside the home. Young children can learn a second language relatively easily. And there was never a question that this would be too difficult for Ariel. Immersed in an English-speaking nursery school, he had no choice but to learn to communicate in the language spoken around him. Ariel's first language (Hebrew) did not detract from his ability to learn to speak and read his second language (English). What actually happened was that with time, English, the language spoken with friends and at school, took over, becoming the dominant language for him.

I cannot fully agree with Diane Barone's statement that "[i]n general, children who cannot claim English as their first language have difficulty achieving academic success in U.S. schools."[15] Children of Asian immigrants are doing very well in our schools. My personal experience in my own family also negates Barone's claim. And it is worthwhile to recall that it used to be customary for affluent families in previous generations (some still do it today) to hire tutors (sometimes foreign-language-speaking nannies) to teach their children a foreign language from an early age, to broaden their education. So there are other reasons for non-English-speaking children to fall behind in U.S. schools. Lack of family confidence in the new country and holding back the children to the old language for fear of losing them to the dominant new culture could be two possible explanations.

In short, bilingualism should be viewed as an advantage rather than a disadvantage. On a practical level, it enables one to communicate with people in other countries. From an educational standpoint, it enhances a child's mental development, increasing synaptogenesis (the formation of connection between brain cells), thereby enriching the brain's operational capacity. "It is clear that brain development results from the interaction of genes and environmental experiences, that growth and elaboration of the neuronal network during the early years of life are critical to children's knowledge construction," write Bergen and Coscia.[16] Furthermore, the years before age nine are the best years for second language acquisition, say Bergen and Coscia, "[b]ecause the ability to recognize and reproduce sounds of the non-native language diminishes with age."[17] When children who are older than nine years of age learn a second language, they typically retain a heavy accent. But before age nine, they can learn a second, sometimes a third language, without an accent.

Learning to speak and read a second language, in the preschool years, whether naturally or formally, does require a supportive home and/or preschool environment. If the parents do not know any English, they should be encouraged to take English classes in parent education or family literacy programs. This will help their own adjustment to the new country as well as their children's. There is an estimate that "one in every seven children speaks a language other than English as his or her first language," writes Barone.[18] And "[a]lthough the students' first language may vary, these students are coming to U.S. schools with the expectations that they will learn English as well as content knowledge," she adds.[19] Therefore, the utmost effort should be made to help these children learn English, including reading and writing, from the earliest possible age. I think it is a mistake to first teach non-English-speaking children in U.S. schools to read in their native language. Rather than integrating them into the mainstream culture, this will increase their sense of alienation.

NATURAL READERS AND THE ISSUE OF PHONEMIC AWARENESS AND PHONICS

While not germane to our central topic, the issue of phonemic awareness and phonics is one of the hottest topics in beginning reading instruction and preschool literacy development.[20] Natural readers have something to teach us in that respect. And as we shall see, they can even be the arbiters in this hot debate.

Different strategies have been commonly used over the years to teach beginning reading, with basically two competing approaches: code-emphasis, that is, learning to read through phonics, and meaning-emphasis, that is, learning to read through word recognition and emphasis on content. There is a long-standing debate between these two approaches that shifts back and forth in emphasis. During the first half of the twentieth century, word recognition skills and emphasis on content dominated beginning reading programs in American schools. But in 1967, Jeanne Chall, a noted reading instruction researcher, concluded that a code-emphasis beginning reading program was more effective for most children, particularly for low-income children.[21] And the struggle between the two camps has intensified since then, with the code-emphasis having a slight upper hand as this chapter is being written.

With the recent inclusion of preschool literacy development in American education, a central new issue is whether to teach decoding skills to preschoolers. Decoding skills include phonemic awareness—the knowledge that words comprise individual sounds. "Children who acquire this ability are able to hear rhyming words and can segment individual sounds out of words and blend them together again," says Lesley M. Morrow,[22] former president of the International Reading Association. Decoding skills also include learning the alphabetic principle, that is, phonics—"knowing that words are composed of letters and that there is a relationship between the printed letters and spoken sounds. Children who learn letter-sound relationships are better readers than children that do not," adds Morrow.[23] So the issue is whether to teach decoding skills to preschoolers. If so, what skills are necessary, how much time should be spent teaching them, and how should they be taught?

This compounded question is more complicated than it may seem because most American early childhood programs have been traditionally based on free play. Decoding skills, on the other hand, which were, until now, associated with the primary grades, have usually involved direct teacher instruction. And there are valid reasons for this difference. The new emphasis on preschool literacy development thus requires some change in teaching didactics in preschools. And as a result confusion prevails among early childhood educators. Natural readers may show us a way out of this confusion.

As is clearly evident in the documented accounts of the children in this book, they all learned the names of the letters and their sounds at the same time that they began to acquire a sight vocabulary; in other words, they developed phonemic awareness and knowledge of phonics in parallel to acquiring word recognition skills. Intuitively, the children, with their parents' help, used a combination of the two basic approaches to beginning reading development. This learning situation evolved naturally. And it was successful with our young readers—helping them master the reading task early—probably because they did most of it through games. The rich variety of reading-related games these children played helped make the abstract concepts of letter names and their sounds palpable to the minds of three- and four-year-old children. Games—even reading-related games—are essentially a form of play, and play is the most beloved activity of preschool children.

On reflection, all this makes a lot of sense because phonemic awareness and knowledge of phonics require and develop analytic skill, whereas word recognition and attention to content require and sharpen the child's memory. Each of these approaches taps a different part of the brain. By intuitively combining these two approaches, the children were literally firing more brainpower at their reading task, helping their early reading acquisition.

So, yes, preschool children have the mental capacity to acquire phonemic awareness and phonics. As with older children, this helps them with the process of reading acquisition. But preschool children learn best through play. And reading- and writing-related games may be among our best means to create play-based literacy-learning situations for this age group. Natural reading development, which is based on play, can thus stimulate preschoolers' literacy development without compromising the traditional play-oriented philosophy of American early childhood education. More information on play and literacy development, with references to published literature on the topic, will be provided in the next chapter.

Chapter Ten

To Take the Natural Course or Not

Reading is to the mind what exercise is to the body.
—Sir Richard Steele

COULD MANY CHILDREN BECOME NATURAL EARLY READERS?

As concluded in Chapter 9, given similar conditions, most preschool children could probably acquire reading capability. Supporting evidence can be found in other cultures. Most Japanese children, for instance, start learning to read at home by age four without formal instruction, with their mothers' or grandmothers' support.[1] In fact, Japanese mothers are expected to teach their children to read. And by the time they enter primary school, at age six, most Japanese children can read *kana*, the first level of the Japanese script. Also the Jewish people, until the beginning of the twentieth century, used to teach many three-year-old boys to read the Torah (the Pentateuch). Beginning with the alphabet, the child progressively learned words and verses of prayers.[2] And in contemporary, postrevolutionary China, urban parents expect preschool teachers to teach their children reading and writing.[3] Also in Hong Kong, reading and writing development in both Chinese and English is widespread in many preschool programs.

Although English, Japanese, Hebrew, and Chinese have different scripts and grammar, children's intrinsic propensity to learn to read is universal, unfolding at about the same age, very much like their ability to learn to speak. So if most Japanese children can learn to read "naturally" before formal schooling (although they do not use this term), and many Jewish boys used to learn to read at age three, there is no reason why American children cannot do the same. The issue is not whether preschoolers can learn to read but whether they should, and then, what is the best approach to develop this ability.

But for natural reading development to become a widespread phenomenon, American society will have to make certain attitudinal adjustments. It will have to recognize that informal early reading development is possible for many, probably most, preschool children. And parents will have to become more relaxed about early reading development and be willing to support the natural process at home. As we saw in the previous chapter, IRA and NAEYC, the two largest national organizations concerned with the issue, are now calling on all parents and preschool teachers to facilitate the literacy development of children from the earliest age possible.

Yet, as things stand today, many parents are still apprehensive about the topic. Views such as "My four year old was close to reading but I did not want to push her," "She'll learn to read when she wants to," and "He asked me to help him with his books, but I thought I'd better leave it to school" continue to be expressed. And although early reading ability is much more common today, compared to just a few decades ago, many parents are still troubled by thoughts such as "An early reader is going to be bored in school," "You may be creating a problem by helping him learn how to read," and "Early reading development is stressful for young children." Since parents' cooperation is essential in early literacy development, let me discuss common concerns about the topic, and analyze the pros and cons of natural reading acquisition.

IS EARLY READING DEVELOPMENT TOO ABSTRACT FOR PRESCHOOLERS?

Many parents think that reading acquisition is mentally too demanding for most preschoolers—it is too abstract and therefore could be a frustrating, stressful, and even harmful experience for them. This argument can be dismissed based on the Japanese and Jewish experiences. If most Japanese preschoolers can handle the process of reading acquisition, and three-year-old Jewish boys could manage it, early reading development is probably not as difficult as many think. Also the many academically oriented nursery schools that have flourished in this country since the 1960s, teaching youngsters beginning reading and writing, prove this point. And so does the long list of published research indicating that preschool children have the mental capacity to learn to read, with no ill effect.[4] So as stated earlier, it is not a question of whether preschoolers *can* learn to read, but rather whether they *should*. It is also important to find out what learning methodology is the most suited for young children, and where this learning should take place—in a school setting, in the home environment, or in both.

IS PLAY NOT MORE IMPORTANT?

In *How to Choose a Nursery School*, I wrote that "[p]lay is a primary activity of young children, whether they are alone or in company. Whenever two or three children come together, play is sure to follow. It surmounts language barriers and crosses cultural boundaries. It is universal in its appeal to children. Anyone who has observed children at play knows the endless and intense involvement of children with their play. It has always been so in human societies, and vivid descriptions of children at play can be found throughout literature since the beginning of recorded time."[5]

The ancient Greek philosophers Plato and Aristotle recognized the value of children's play. Friedrich Froebel, the founder of the kindergarten system, exalted the role of play in early childhood education. The psychoanalyst Sigmund Freud and his followers found play to be essential for children's emotional well-being. And the renowned psychologists Jean Piaget and Lev Vygotsky developed elaborate theories about play and its importance in early childhood development.[6] The topic continues to attract much attention in current research and education, from different points of interest, one of which is the association between play and the development of young children's literacy.[7]

Play is so basic for children's development that it is often argued that the early years of childhood should be devoted to play activities. That to do otherwise is to deprive children of their childhood. Many early childhood experts consider free play to be particularly important, because it facilitates learning in the physical, social, emotional, and cognitive aspects of young children's growth and development.[8] Because of that recognition, play has been the basic component in the traditional American nursery school (and surprisingly also in the Japanese preschool program[9]).

However, while there is general agreement among early childhood experts, and most parents, about the importance of play, there is little agreement about what constitutes play. This disagreement comes to the fore in particular in a time, such as ours, when there is pressure to pay more attention in the early years to academics. Yet one can argue that when enjoyable reading-and-writing activities spontaneously develop between parents (or teachers) and children, these interactions often take on the nature of play. We all know that play includes not only a physical or socioemotional dimension but often engages mental faculties as well. In fact, one can say that any activity that is spontaneous, enjoyable, self-directed, with no immediate objectives, and that can be terminated at will is a form of play. In this sense, play ranges from a preschooler's activity with blocks—constructing, for example, a highway system on the kitchen floor—to a scientist experimenting (playing) with a new laboratory tool, or designing a new theoretical model on his or her computer.

Therefore, silly rhyme making and other spontaneous letter-sound games, finding missing letters in words, writing a grocery list, reading to a doll, or forming words with magnetic letters on the refrigerator door are all forms of play, as long as the child enjoys the activity and can terminate it at his or her will. The fact that these activities are associated with reading and writing does not detract from their play quality. And as long as they maintain their play quality, such activities are not stressful or harmful to young children—mentally or emotionally. As Kathleen Roskos and James Christie write in the afterword to their book, "At play, young children can encounter, manipulate, and/or practice a wide range of literacy concepts and related processes that may benefit their individual literacy development and ultimately their literacy achievement."[10]

COULD EARLY READING ABILITY CAUSE DEFICIENCIES IN OTHER AREAS OF DEVELOPMENT?

Some parents and early childhood experts are concerned that early reading ability could adversely affect a child's development in other important areas of growth; that it will divert the child's attention from more important early childhood activities. They worry that early readers will end up deficient in their social, emotional, or physical development. Even worse, that they will become candidates for early burnout.[11]

There is absolutely no indication from available research that early reading ability is harmful to children in any way or manner. On the contrary, early readers appear to develop as happily as nonreaders do. The early reading ability, by itself, does not affect their social or emotional development in any negative fashion, any more than an early swimming ability, an early bilingual ability, or an early ability to play the violin (following the Suzuki method). One can argue that these children's success in acquiring a desirable skill may even add to their sense of self-esteem. As for future academic development, numerous anecdotal reports, as well as a couple of studies,[12] indicate that early readers continue to maintain their advantage in reading ability in later years, a fact that must also add to their sense of confidence and self-esteem. (My own two early-reading sons, for example, grew up to become a successful pediatrician and a top-ranking earth scientist.)

It is noteworthy to keep in mind that early reading acquisition does not require more than a total of about a half hour a day with a parent or other significant adult (and this time could be made up of several short segments). More time could of course be devoted, as shown in the examples of the children described in this book, but this is not necessary. But even if close to two hours a day were devoted to a child's literacy development (this will include an educational television program, some computer software, and daily readings to the child), there will still be plenty of time left over for all the other important childhood activities.

There will be time to do puzzles, build sand castles, do art projects, work with blocks, ride a tricycle, play in the park, go shopping with Mom or Dad, play cops and robbers with siblings or friends, or attend a preschool program.

So, an interest in literacy does not exclude other areas of interest. It certainly does not consume all of a child's life. If early readers turn out to experience some problems in later years (and there is no reason why they should be different in this respect than the rest of the population of children), the causes of that problem will be unrelated to their early reading ability.

EARLY READING ACQUISITION AND BRAIN DEVELOPMENT

Will early reading development affect general mental capacity? This is a hot question with far-reaching implications. It is the engine behind the new changes in policy toward early literacy. As new brain-imaging technologies enable scientists to investigate brain function, former hypotheses regarding the early years' importance for children's mental development are being confirmed. For example, Julee Newberger, in an article for *Young Children*, the most widely read professional journal of early childhood education, made the following statement:

> We now know that during the early years the brain has the greatest capacity for change. Neural plasticity, the brain's ability to adapt with experience, confirms that early stimulation sets the stage for how children will continue to learn and interact with others throughout life. . . . Particularly during the first three years of life, brain connections develop quickly in response to outside stimulation. A child's experiences—good or bad—influence the wiring of his brain and the connections in his nervous system.[13]

In other words, when the infant is born, most of its brain cells are not yet functional. Individual brain cells, the neurons, are separate, and connections (synapses) between the neurons have first to form to give the brain its capacity to function. Microscopic photographs show that as the child grows, the brain cells form connections from one cell to another (axons and dendrites) like bridges, to respond to and correlate information received from the outside through the senses. Sensory stimulation and perception lead to the formation of new connections between these cells. As these connections sprout and develop, the capacity of the brain increases. "It is clear that brain development results from the interaction of genes and environmental experiences, that growth and elaboration of the neuronal network during the early years of life are critical to children's knowledge construction," write Doris Bergen and Juliet Coscia in *Brain Research and Childhood Education.*[14]

Experiments on rats, for example, show that when the cortex (the "thinking" part of the brain) was stimulated in an enriched environment by toys such as ladders, slides, trapezes, blocks, wheels, and brushes, its actual size changed compared to the brains of unstimulated rats, living in a bare environment. The cortex of the stimulated rats thickened and weighed more than the cortex of unstimulated rats. The number of brain cells did not increase but the cell bodies became larger, and the branches between the cells proliferated with increased density of points of contact between the cells.[15]

These observations from brain research indicate that rather than being fixed and predetermined, neural mechanisms are responsive to and capable of being shaped by a variety of external factors. These research findings match so well studies in child development and early education that it prompted Howard Gardner, the noted educational psychologist, to state that "[t]he effects of enrichment and deprivation conditions can now be demonstrated by measuring the size of brain regions, number or density of synaptic connections, and other relatively hard measures of neural organizations."[16]

Now, the period between birth to age three (the same period when natural reading acquisition begins to emerge and develop) is the period when brain cells make, most rapidly, branches and connections between cells. There is evidence that synaptic density is highest in these early years, followed by a period of pruning and reduction, until a more limited adult cell level is reached. This finding strengthens the viewpoint that the first three years of life are a critical period for learning, one in which the foundation is laid for all future mental operations. This finding also fits well with Benjamin Bloom's 1964 statement that

50 percent of a person's IQ potential is developed by age four and 80 percent by age eight.[17]

Will early literacy activities contribute to the formation of connections between brain cells? Bergen and Coscia respond:

> A body of research evidence supports the view that the earliest years of life (ages 1 to 4) are the optimum time for extensive development of oral language, especially in regards to phonological and syntactical rule learning. . . . Research also indicates that emerging literacy skills begin to develop in infancy . . . there appears to be a sensitive period in which such skills develop more easily, and evidence points to a genetic/environment interaction that promotes such development.[18]

There is little doubt that such activities stimulate the sensory system and challenge the child to think. "All educational practices that expand learning experiences and challenge thinking can be influences on brain growth and neurological development, because brains are in part 'created' by each individual," add Bergen and Coscia.[19] Moreover, if pruning of synaptic connections already begins around age three, it makes sense to assume that early reading activities will maintain connections that would be lost otherwise, enriching the brain's mental capacity. And, conversely, connections already formed may degenerate if they are not further activated.

It is also important to keep in mind that since speech and reading—the oral and written aspects of language—have much in common, the period that is most conducive for the development of speech may also be the period most conducive for the initial development of reading. John Eccles and Daniel Robinson write that "[b]oth cerebral hemispheres participate in speech initially. Normally the left hemisphere gradually becomes dominant in speech performance, both in interpretation and in expression. . . . Meanwhile, the other hemisphere, usually the right, is repressed in respect to speech production but retains some competence in understanding. This process of speech transfer is usually complete by four or five years of age."[20]

It is possible that both cerebral hemispheres, each with its unique operational characteristics, is needed to enable the toddler to grasp the symbolic aspect of language. Once the young child has mastered the concept of language, a part of the brain has fulfilled its function, is no longer needed, and can slowly atrophy. (For if the initial capacity of the right hemisphere to participate in speech development was not needed, why would it be there to begin with, and why would it begin to atrophy around age four or five?) The right hemispheric area involved in speech development may also be helpful for beginning reading acquisition.

This idea is not new. It has been proposed by Robert Lado, Ragnhild Soderbergh, George Stevens and W. E. Amos,[21] as well as several other linguists who recommended years ago that reading acquisition should go hand in hand with the development of speech; namely, that in the period when spoken language is acquired, the child has a special capacity for absorbing all aspects of language.

Additional evidence for higher linguistic brain capacity in the early years of life can be derived from the known fact that second language acquisition is much easier before age six than later. Preschoolers can easily become bilingual, compared to adults, mastering both their native and their second language without developing an accent. Older children, on the other hand, as well as adults, find second language acquisition much more difficult and they typically develop a heavy accent.

"What is it about young children's brains that makes them so good at absorbing language?" asks the neurobiologist Lise Eliot in her engaging book *What's Going On in There?* "Why is a newer, immature brain so immensely better at learning grammar and mastering pronunciation than an older, smarter one? Once again, the answer is in the remarkable plasticity of the young nervous system. Brains learn by resculpting their synapses and dendrites, and early life, when the number of synapses in a child's brain is at its peak, presents the greatest opportunity for selecting the optimal neural pathways for mediating language," writes Eliot.[22]

In conclusion, early reading activities may draw on the preschool child's special capacity for language; possibly making beginning reading acquisition in the early years easier than at a later age. This is a speculative idea at this point in time, but it is hard to reject the hypothesis that early literacy activities contribute to the formation of new connections between brain cells; at the minimum, these activities will increase the child's mental capacity. And there is much observational evidence to substantiate this claim. On the other hand, as Bergen and Coscia write, research suggests that a paucity of "cognitive-language stimulation in the infant and toddler years may retard optimum brain growth and neurological functioning."[23] This realization is one of the engines behind the new initiative for preschool literacy development. So, until new findings from brain research add more facts to our educational theory, one can conclude that there appear to be both physiological and educational justifications for developmentally appropriate early reading development.

WILL EARLY READERS BE BORED IN SCHOOL?

Another common concern regarding early reading development is school-related. Some parents hesitate to stimulate a youngster's interests in reading for fear that an early ability will cause problems in grade school. "It is not so much the case that many children have difficulties with learning to read in kindergarten, but rather that many children know too much," reflected one kindergarten teacher. This has been a concern when the educational establishment was opposed to early reading. But with the recent policy changes toward preschool literacy, this issue is invalid. Indeed, what will happen to an early reader once he or she begins formal schooling? Will that child be bored?

There are several ways a teacher could handle the accelerated ability of an early reader who starts formal schooling. For example, if a number of children in a given classroom have similar advanced reading skills, they could form the more advanced group among the different reading groups that exist in most primary-grade classrooms. If only one child is significantly ahead of the rest of the class, he or she may receive individualized instruction—after school or during quiet work time—from the teacher, an aid, a volunteer, a neighborhood "grandparent," or even a child from a higher grade. Another possibility is to send such a child to a higher grade for his or her reading period. These are just a few examples of possible arrangements that would ensure the continued development of an early reader, preventing potential boredom. Other accommodations could probably also be arranged.

I cannot emphasize enough the importance of continuing to develop the advanced reading skills of an early reader, irrespective of how proficient he or she may be. If a teacher ignores it, neglecting to give the child the necessary stimulation to further his or her literacy skills, that child's development may indeed be stifled. Self-esteem may get hurt, and rather than continue to progress, that child may slow down or even regress. On the other hand, it would be just as wrong to discourage a preschooler's interest in print—suppressing the child's development—for fear that the school system will fail to provide future individualized attention. This will contradict all our knowledge about young children's development. Parents can collaborate with teachers to ensure optimal development.

In any case, since the number of children entering school with some knowledge of reading is growing, schools will have to accommodate children's individualized reading needs. Different school districts will try different approaches (many are already doing that), and primary-grade teachers will be increasingly prepared to work with children entering school with different degrees of reading and writing ability.

SHOULD READING ACQUISITION BE A PRESCHOOL OBJECTIVE?

If preschoolers have the capacity to learn how to read, why shouldn't early childhood teachers take on the responsibility and teach them reading? (I focus on reading and not writing because many three- and four-year-olds' finger dexterity and eye/hand coordination is not yet developed enough for conventional writing.) This is a valid question and parents are increasingly bringing it up. And the educational establishment is carefully moving in the direction of literacy development. But I emphasize *beginning* reading and writing development. Not reading acquisition.

In fact, some preschool teachers working in academically oriented programs have been teaching reading to three- and four-year-old children since the 1960s.[24] But generally speaking, these programs have not gained much popularity with the American public. And the educational establishment has shied away from endorsing these programs. The majority of preschool teachers and parents have strong long-standing feelings against structured preschool programs that emphasize academics. Although many parents sense, even know, that their preschoolers are ready for reading, they have a gut feeling that academically oriented programs do not provide the best environment for their preschool child.

What are the reasons for this intuitive objection? Simply put, academic objectives, namely, teaching preschoolers reading, writing, and mathematics, *systematically*, in a group setting, require formal instruction, and an assessment of progress. Many preschool children, while mentally capable of developing beginning literacy, are not yet ready for the structure and discipline that is required for group instruction. They do not have the neurological maturation to focus and sit still long enough to learn and wait for the rest of the children in their group—when they are not particularly interested. They are more impatient than older children are. They like to be on the go. And we must also remember that children learn at different rates. Some are quick and some are slow.

Furthermore, since the pace of children's learning varies, many parents and early childhood teachers are reluctant to expose preschoolers to the pressure of academic assessment. They are concerned about early labeling and typecasting—particularly at a period in life in which abilities are not yet fixed. It is soon enough, they say, to begin with that in the primary grades. The preschool years should be devoted to other, not less important, learning tasks—in the social, emotional, physical, and general cognitive domains, they say.

For all these reasons, most parents and early childhood teachers feel more comfortable with the traditional American early childhood program that (while appearing under different names) emphasizes play activities. Yet, this attitude is now changing. With the new reading legislation, and the recent realization of the critical importance of early literacy for children's mental development and later scholastic achievements, objectives of early childhood education are being reformulated. And more attention will be given to literacy development.

The purpose of this book is to demonstrate to parents and teachers—through the stories of the six children—how it is possible to stimulate the natural reading development of preschool children without direct, systematic instruction: playfully learning the names of the letters and their sounds; playfully developing in children recognition of words in the environment; dramatizing popular stories and life situations that involve the printed word (such as shopping in a grocery store, going to the doctor's office, pretending to be a teacher); and singing songs, making rhymes, and engaging in varied spontaneous and playful literacy activities that are embedded in children's lives, on their level of understanding and interest. When such activities are continuously engaged in, literacy will be stimulated and encouraged *informally*. It will then be developmentally appropriate, following a natural course of development. Preschool children love to play. Even if that play involves letters, sounds, and words. Moreover, play can be repetitive. Preschoolers enjoy playing a good game over and over again. And so slower children will have the time to catch up with the faster children.

So, should reading acquisition become an objective for preschool programs? Absolutely not. Beginning literacy development should be the goal for preschools—informally, naturally—with each child learning at his or her pace and stage of development. Some children will be slower and some will be faster. This is true of all age levels but particularly so at the preschool stage. More specific guidebooks for early childhood teachers on how to encourage preschool children's literacy development will be available soon.

But while preschool teachers cannot have reading acquisition as an objective in their programs, parents will have an increasing role to play in their preschool children's literacy development, collaborating with the teachers to promote the natural literacy development of their youngsters. As Stephen R. Burgess, Steven A. Hecht, and Christopher J. Lonigan write, "The race to identify effective methods of manipulating the HLE (Home Literacy Environment) has begun. Educators, politicians, and parents are demanding higher educational achievement. . . . One of the areas of greatest untapped potential is the home."[25] There are things that parents can do that teachers cannot. And that will be the focus of the discussion in the following section.

THE EDUCATIONAL UNIQUENESS OF THE HOME ENVIRONMENT

Natural reading acquisition, as illustrated throughout this book, is qualitatively very different from formal reading instruction. Instead of following a prescribed adult-directed methodology, natural reading development unfolds around children's interests. Rather than being taught by an adult, natural reading acquisition is child-centered. This is a learning process that emerges from within the child in a responsive environment. Natural reading acquisition is nonsystematic, whereas formal reading instruction is systematic and predetermined. The child is an active learner rather than being passively taught and drilled. Playfulness and spontaneity are key characteristics of natural reading development. Freedom to step in and out of a learning activity is another key component. And the one-to-one interaction between child and adult is an all-important feature. For all these reasons, natural reading acquisition is the most child-oriented reading development process. It is the most suited for the preschool age. And when it is individualized, it is the best, and the most fitting, reading program for the home environment.

When a child's reading-related experiences are sensitively based on that child's interests, and are matched with his or her ability, these experiences are developmentally appropriate. And when interesting literacy activities are neither difficult nor frustrating, not too easy or boring, they can cause neither mental nor emotional harm.

Moreover, when reading-related experiences are child-centered, the learning process is likely to be efficient as well as pleasant. Little time will be wasted on activities that are not suited for the child, and from which he or she will not learn. When parents take their cues from their child's questions and reading interests, responding at the child's level of understanding, there is no need to worry about a "correct" order of development. That youngster's interests will be determined by his or her own natural timetable, and the parents will be facilitating the natural course of development of that child.

"The years from the crib to the classroom represent a period of intense language and cognitive growth," writes William Teale.[26] And the process of natural reading acquisition can begin in the first year of life. It may start before most children even attend an early childhood program. Many natural readers are independent readers by the time they start a preschool program. Establishing a literate home environment is, therefore, even more important for the stimulation of children's early literacy than the most literate environment in an early childhood center.

There is another important feature characteristic of the home environment that makes it especially conducive for natural reading development. A curious preschooler is more likely to experience spontaneous reading events in a home rich with age-appropriate print than under the group care of a teacher who may not be able to attend to his or her particular reading interest at a particular moment. "What does it say?" "What does this say?" "How do you spell it?" "What's the name of this letter?" or "Please read me this story!" are typical requests of two- and three-year-old children in a literate home environment. Such incidental learning can go on also outside the home—reading road signs during walks around the block, direction words inside a mall, names of stores, and so on. The same child may have only limited opportunity to ask these questions of a busy preschool teacher surrounded by many children.

In addition, children in a literate home environment may engage in reading-related activities not only to satisfy a mental interest or negotiate a particular life experience, but also as a means to impress their parents and attract their attention. Since parents can give children individualized attention, much more than a teacher, children may often feel more rewarded at home for their reading attempts. This positive feeling may then increase their interest in reading.

And as for working parents, with less time at home, could they still facilitate their children's natural reading development? As we saw in Carrie's story (Chapter 4), working parents can also create a literate home environment. They can stimulate and support their children's reading interests whenever they share some time together. It is all a matter of attitude and readiness to encourage the children's reading interest.

As was said earlier, the process of natural reading development does not require much more than a half hour a day of work time with one or both parents. Working parents often try to compensate for the time they are away from their preschoolers.

Feeling the need to emphasize quality over quantity, they may show greater interest in reading-related activities with their children. Besides, career-minded parents are often more ambitious for their children. Wishing to prepare them for academic excellence, they may engage them more often in literacy-related activities from an early age.

So, if working parents have the energy and desire, they can stimulate their children's natural reading development just as much as a stay-at-home parent does. A babysitter, nanny, family day-care provider, or a teacher can add support to the learning process. The following anecdote related by a day-care teacher is a beautiful illustration of good cooperation between home and school: Having a four-year-old reader in his group, a teacher asked the boy's mother one day, "Who taught Charlie to read?" "I do not know," replied the mother. "You taught some, we taught some, and between us he picked up the necessary skills."

TO TAKE THE NATURAL PATH OR NOT

If you read this book up to this point, you will now probably pause and reflect on whether to take the natural course or not, whether it is worthwhile to invest all that time and effort to encourage young children's natural reading development. Let me try to be of help. There is no doubt in my mind that natural reading development will encourage young children's reading ability and stimulate their general mental capacity. The educational establishment is now recommending the literacy development of all preschool children.

All the knowledge we have gained about child development and early learning, knowledge that has been accumulated over years of professional experience and educational, psychological, and brain research, clearly points in one direction. When young children show interest in letters, words, sounds of letters, or any other print-related matter, they are open and ready to learn. Moreover, they are then in their best learning mode. As the neuropsychologist Ursula Kirk writes, "It is the active learner who learns; passivity characterizes the child who does not learn."[27] Parents can always stimulate and encourage children's interest and development. That is in your hands, every day, at every moment that you share with your child. Don't dull your child's mental potential by brushing him or her off for being too young, for fear of causing harm, or for lack of time.

Although teachers in traditional play-oriented preschool programs cannot provide the same daily individualized attention as parents or other in-home caregivers, they can create a literate environment in their center that will stimulate and support the children's natural learning process. They can do this informally, through games, dramatic play, environmental print, and numerous other print activities (as illustrated in the children's stories) that will encourage literacy development. Good traditional programs have been increasingly doing that, and with the mounting pressure for early literacy development, they will continue to advance in that direction.

And preschool teachers have another unique role. They can provide the necessary support and guidance to parents about how to encourage children's natural reading development at home. As Matthew Melmed of ZERO TO THREE, a Washington-based national organization dedicated to advancing the healthy development of young children, writes, "Many parents of young children may need guidance if they are to maximize experiences in the early years. What they lack is not just information on the importance of the earliest years but also specific steps, ideas, activities, and concepts for making the most of this time."[28] Michelle Porche, a research analyst at the Harvard Graduate School of Education, puts it even more directly: "Teachers can take the initiative by providing guidance to parents in emphasizing reading activities with children."[29] Together, parents and teachers could stimulate many, if not most, children's early literacy development. Preschool teachers could thus contribute to children's natural reading development without compromising the underlying philosophy of the traditional American early childhood program that is based on play.

THE LONG-TERM PERSPECTIVE

Natural early reading development is a challenge. It is a mental challenge for young children, but I do not think that it is a greater challenge than learning to speak. (A spoken word is a symbol not any less than a written word.) It is a challenge for parents. But if they enjoy stimulating their children's mental faculties, they will be rewarded. They may also establish a stronger bond with their children, who will surely enjoy learning to read on their parents' lap much more so than in the more formal school environment. But perhaps most importantly, natural reading development is a challenge for American society, and the educational establishment.

Imagine the implications for the educational system if a growing number of children learn to read naturally in their preschool years. It may increase the disparity between children whose reading development is encouraged at home and those who are not stimulated at home (a disparity that already exists to a smaller degree). It could highlight the gap between the rich and the poor, and between children from two-parent versus single-parent homes, unless all parents, from all socioeconomic backgrounds, are guided on how to encourage the literacy development of their children at home. Schools will have to cope with that situation and orchestrate how best to advance all groups of children. (Perhaps we can learn something from the Japanese. As we saw earlier, Japanese mothers are expected to teach their preschoolers to read, informally, while the preschool program is devoted to play activities and socialization skills.)

America as a nation must never stop striving for the highest possible educational achievements of its children. We cannot permit ourselves to lower our standards to the lowest common denominator. If other societies continue to strive for excellence (the Japanese or the Chinese, for example), how can we do any less?

The world is in a continuous process of change (i.e., evolution). It feels much smaller today and much more competitive. The economic base of this nation has changed. America today is in a serious global competition on many fronts. The winning society in the future will be the one that is strongest, not necessarily in military terms (as important as that may be) or in the amount of its natural resources or other material goods, but the strongest in its brainpower. The winning society will be the one most able to discover and create new technologies that will provide an increasingly growing population with meaningful and productive employment opportunities. The winning society will also create a twenty-first-century way of life that will develop a citizenry with the highest degree of health—both physical and emotional—and the resulting contentment with life. Large-scale natural early reading development, with its likely positive effect on children's mental development, may bring us closer to that goal.

Chapter Eleven

———————

How, When, and Where

"Tony," says five-year-old Mike to his older brother by 15 months, who was an accomplished reader prior to entering kindergarten. "I don't get this! How do you do it?" Now a seasoned first grader with one full week of experience, Tony says wisely, "Oh, Mike, don't worry. It's easy! You see, you just sit on mom's lap and she reads you stories. Then you can read the words."

—adapted from N. Lynne Decker Collins and
Margaret B. Shaeffer, "Look, Listen,
and Learn to Read"

THE PARENTS' ROLE

Once you have decided to try natural reading development with your child, how do you go about it? If you read through the children's stories in the previous chapters, you have probably developed an idea of how to approach the topic. Follow your intuition. Remember that you are your child's first and most important teacher. You know better than anyone else does what your child likes and what he or she does not like. You know better than anyone else your child's interests, and, most important, when he or she is ready to start learning the beginnings of reading and writing.

The following pages offer a summary list of recommendations rather than a prescription. You can adopt all of these ideas, or pick and choose. The key point to remember is that natural reading development is most likely to emerge when you share interesting and *enjoyable* print-related experiences with your child on a daily basis. But do not expect to see immediate results. Remember that we are dealing with a developmental step-by-step process.

Some Attitudinal Preconditions

To begin with, there are several attitudinal preconditions that need to be taken into consideration:

1. You have to be open to the possibility of natural reading development. Only when you accept this possibility, will you provide your child with the necessary stimulation and encouragement essential for the emergence of the process.

2. You have to feel comfortable with the idea of early reading development before you can start to facilitate it. Your child may sense any apprehension on your part regarding the topic and withdraw from the reading experience. Preschoolers are keen psychologists. They are very sensitive to their parents' feelings, and have a fine ability to detect slight nuances. If your child senses (or possibly overhears) that you think he or she is too young for reading, or that you worry about possible negative side effects, that child's excitement about reading may dampen and he or she may refuse to give the process his or her best mental effort. Talk out any concerns you may have about this process with a knowledgeable person before you attempt to encourage it.

3. It is important to realize that the encouragement of natural reading development will not require a substantial amount of your time. It may appear from the six children's stories that the parents spent much time on reading activities with those children. But remem-

ber that these accounts were presented in a very concentrated fashion. The spotlight was on reading. But many other things were happening in these children's lives all along. Natural reading development is a long-term process (lasting about eighteen months, from stage 2 to stage 7), and it requires some daily attention. But so will any other reading acquisition process; including reading development in the primary grades. At its best, natural reading development should be embedded in preschoolers' routine daily activities, encouraged spontaneously several times a day with a few moments here and there devoted to each literacy interaction. Once you realize that about a half hour a day suffices to facilitate this process, you will have the necessary patience to persist with it.

4. Spontaneity, playfulness, creativity, intuition, and continuity with literacy interactions will encourage natural reading development and keep the process alive. These same qualities will also make the process enjoyable for you and for your child.

5. It is important that both parents share the same philosophical orientation toward natural reading development, giving the same message to the child. If one parent tries to encourage natural reading development while the other thinks the child is not yet ready for reading and withdraws his or her support (either passively or actively), the child may choose to identify with the discouraging parent and shrink from the reading experience.

6. Never measure and never pressure. That is best left for formal schooling. Irrespective of how fast your child's reading development evolves, make literacy a pleasant experience in your household. Be patient and persistent and rest assured that your child will benefit from that experience.

7. Remember that you have nothing to lose by trying this process. There are absolutely no negative side effects to it. And you can stop it at any time.

8. Also keep in mind that natural reading acquisition deals only with the preschool age. We are not discussing here

reading development in the primary grades. Once an early reader enters the first grade, that child's teacher will continue to develop the child's ability from whatever level he or she is at. Early readers usually continue to do very well in grade school.

Practical Recommendations

In addition to these attitudinal preconditions, there are a number of practical steps you can take to stimulate the natural reading development of your child:

1. Arrange from year one a literate home environment. This means, first of all, a good selection of stimulating, age-appropriate picture books, including, for instance, cardboard books, cloth books, plastic books, and touch-and-feel books for the infancy period. There are many concept books, including the alphabet, numbers, colors, body parts, animals, and nursery rhymes, for the toddler age. For older preschoolers, you can find a large selection of picture storybooks, fairy tales, and easy-to-read books. Read these books to your child from year one. And let the child handle favorite books by himself or herself. It is important not to overload the child, especially at the infancy stage, with too many new books at a time. Overstimulation may unnerve the child and cause a loss of interest. It is also important to match new books with the child's level of comprehension. If books are too easy, they could bore the child, and if they are too difficult, they may turn the child off. A mix of books, some with limited text to develop the child's reading confidence and some with more developed text to enrich the child's vocabulary, concepts, and imagination, is a good idea.

2. Read to your child daily from these books, pointing at the words. Some parents begin reading to their children from day one (occasionally even before the child is born). It is a good idea to make reading a home ritual, practiced at the same time and in the same place

every day, on top of all the incidental readings that may occur throughout the day in response to a child's request. In many homes, bedtime is a favorite time for reading. And bedtime stories are a nice habit to establish. It helps create a warm bond between parent and child, which will last a lifetime for both parent and child to cherish. It is important to engage children in simple discussions following a book reading, responding to their questions about the pictures or the content. This will develop their thinking ability and improve their comprehension.

3. Develop a habit of pointing out environmental print to your child from an early age, such as labels on familiar cereal boxes, ice-cream containers, and other food packages; direction words on kitchen appliances such as ON or OFF, or IN, OUT, and EXIT in department stores. Ask your child to help you find a needed number in the telephone book, a new recipe in your cookbook, a favorite program in the television guide, or an advertisement in the newspaper. When outdoors, point out to your child road signs, street names, and names of fast-food restaurants, gas stations, and chain stores. Occasionally spotlight the letters. Pointing out and drawing attention to words and letters in the environment will develop your child's awareness of print. It will sharpen his or her visual memory and stimulate natural reading development.

4. A literate home environment will provide children with access to basic materials that encourage early literacy development. These include unlined white paper (the older the child, the smaller the sheets can be) and different writing tools, including pencils, crayons, markers, and a chalkboard with chalk. Older infants should, of course, be supervised with these materials and shown their proper use. Have attractive alphabet letters, including magnetic letters and letter blocks, available to your child to play/practice prereading and writing activities. An assortment of reading-related toys and games, puzzles with words, and, if you can afford it, electronic reading games are also important.

Appropriately designed computer software will also be useful. All of these materials should be carefully matched with the child's level of ability at the time they are introduced. This will maximize the child's sense of success with the developmental reading and writing process. Once again, it is important to keep things in proportion and not overstimulate the child with too many toys and games at a time.

5. Be sensitive to your child's interests, and create literacy events around these, responding as much as you can to his or her queries. Make your print interactions as exciting as possible. As demonstrated in the children's stories, be creative and adopt or invent reading- and writing-related games. These games should be as enjoyable as other types of games. A game is a game. While a ball game will exercise and develop the child's muscles and bones, reading and writing games will exercise and develop the child's brain and mental faculty, as well as eye/hand coordination and fine finger dexterity. To recognize familiar words in a newspaper can be as exciting for a two- or three-year-old child as articulating a new word. Finding missing letters in words can be as much fun as playing hide-and-seek games. Many types of games can contribute to a child's wholesome development.

6. Expose your child, from an early age, to *Sesame Street* or other age-appropriate educational television, video, or computer programs oriented toward children's literacy development. You can do this even more than once a day—for a short period—if your child is asking for a particular program, at a particular phase of development. These programs can be of benefit as long as you keep them in balance with all of the other activities your child must engage in. Watch some programs with your youngster, discussing selected segments, asking questions, and raising a critical issue to develop your child's thinking ability.

7. Do not worry about "the correct" order of literacy stimulation. As long as these interactions are conducted with sensitivity to the child's level of understanding, and are playful in nature and with no

pressure, they are developmentally appropriate. As long as the child enjoys the reading or writing activity, it can do no harm. At each phase, the child will absorb whatever he or she needs in order to continue and progress in his or her developmental process of natural reading development. Remember that your role is to stimulate and encourage, but the process of development will be determined by the child's brain. The key to natural reading development is the child's interest and enjoyment in engaging in literacy activities and interactions.

THE PRESCHOOL TEACHER'S ROLE

Let me now address the preschool teacher. A probable critique you will level at me is that all the examples in this book are of children with a stay-at-home mom, with the exception of Carrie who had a nanny. With so many preschoolers attending daylong childcare, why did I not include one of these children, demonstrating how that child acquired natural reading development? Does it apply only to children with a stay-at-home mom? you will ask.

Well, until the recent call to early childhood educators, by IRA and NAEYC, to encourage the literacy development of *all* children from the earliest possible age, the prevailing attitude was to not do much about reading and writing development with preschoolers. The emphasis in the majority of preschool programs was on play. The common notion was that reading and writing activities are developmentally inappropriate for the preschool age. Therefore, most early readers used to be kids with a stay-at-home mom (or a good substitute) especially during their early preschool years. But this situation has now changed. With the new recommendations of the educational establishment, I predict that we will increasingly see early readers also among children who attend daylong preschool. It is important to remember that natural reading development is, to a large extent, based on play. It can therefore be easily incorporated into the play-oriented traditional American early education program.

While natural reading development is ideal for the home environment, because of the individualized attention and one-to-one interaction possible there, you can encourage this development also at the preschool environment. What you cannot offer in terms of much individualized attention, you can compensate for by providing guidance to parents on how to develop natural reading development at home. Parents and teachers together could facilitate this development for most, if not all, children. Teachers have a tremendous opportunity here, in particular with families in which both parents work outside the home.

All of my recommendations to parents also apply to preschool teachers:

- Create a highly literate preschool environment.
- Believe that natural reading development is possible.
- Draw the children's attention to words and letters in the environment.
- Use literacy-oriented games and activities in your program, highlighting words, letters, and their sounds. The six children's stories are filled with good ideas. Additional resources can be found in, for example, *Games for Reading* by Peggy Kay; *Growing Up Reading—Learning to Read through Creative Play* by Jill Frankel Hauser; *Literacy through Play* by Gretchen Owocki; *Play and Literacy in Early Childhood*, edited by Kathleen A. Roskos and James F. Christie; and "Engaging Preschoolers in Code Learning" by Judith A. Schickedanz.[1]
- Make literacy activities an enjoyable experience.
- Be spontaneous and creative with reading and writing activities.
- Stimulate and encourage, but do not pressure. Remember that each child has his or her own pace of development.
- You can certainly assess children's progress, but do it at this stage, informally. *Kidwatching* by Gretchen Owocki and Yetta Goodman offers guidance on how to do that.[2]

Overall, treat natural reading development, whether at home or at preschool, in a similar fashion to children's speech development. As Ken Goodman says, "Oral- and written-language processes work in much the same way and they are learned in much the same way. . . .Written language shares all the characteristics of oral language except that it's visual rather than aural. We perceive it with our eyes, not our ears. . . . Reading is language, no less and no more than listening is language. People learn both in the same ways and for the same reasons."[3] So stimulate, encourage, model, support, coach, and play, responding to children's literacy interests with patience and enthusiasm. Preschoolers' curiosity and drive to learn can indeed be exhausting, but keep in mind that children at this age are in a highly active stage of development—physically, emotionally, and mentally.

Research indicates that most U.S. children today, even those growing up in inner-city neighborhoods, experience repeated reading- and writing-related interactions in their homes before formal schooling. It is possible that in the contemporary literate environment many children actually begin the process of natural reading development—perhaps even mastering the first two or three stages—as may be indicated by the growing number of children entering kindergarten with some knowledge of reading. However, as discussed in the previous chapter, many parents may not encourage the process all the way. They may lose patience. They may lack confidence to proceed beyond the most elementary level. They may fear doing something wrong. Or, unaware that their simple activities may eventually lead to reading, they may not persist with them. And many working parents may simply be too tired to stimulate their children's development. But with the new realization of the importance of preschool literacy development this situation will change. And teachers will have an important role in rectifying this condition.

CONCLUSION

Whenever the doors to literacy are opened, youngsters will happily walk in. The stories of the children in this book demonstrate different styles of stimulating natural reading development. You have the freedom to choose and create what is best for each child. The bottom line is that parents can literally open children's eyes and minds to the world of literacy from an early age. Once a child goes to preschool, teachers can add their stimulation and encouragement.

Notes

CHAPTER 1: READING HAS A HISTORY

1. Denise Schmandt-Besserat, *How Writing Came About* (Austin: University of Texas Press, 1992), 15–25.
2. Cited in Felix Reichmann, *The Sources of Western Literacy* (Westport, CT: Greenwood, 1980), 53.
3. Ibid., 12.
4. Will Durant, *The Story of Civilization,* vol. 1 (New York: Simon and Schuster, 1954), 76.
5. Geoffrey Sampson, *Writing Systems* (Stanford, CA: Stanford University Press, 1985), 172–192.
6. Andrew Robinson, *The Story of Writing* (London: Thames and Hudson, 1995), 159.
7. Cited in Nila Banton Smith, *American Reading Instruction* (Newark, DE: International Reading Association, 1986), 11.
8. Ibid., 426.

CHAPTER 2: WHEN DO CHILDREN LEARN TO READ?

1. Cited in Edward E. Gordon and Elaine H. Gordon, *Literacy in America* (Westport, CT: Praeger, 2003), 93.
2. Ibid., 94.

3. Ibid., 28.

4. Edmund B. Huey, *The Psychology and Pedagogy of Reading* (New York: Macmillan, 1908; Cambridge, MA: MIT Press, 1968), 379. Citations are to the MIT edition.

5. Ibid., 313.

6. Gordon and Gordon, *Literacy in America*, 109–110.

7. Dolores Durkin, *Getting Reading Started* (Boston: Allyn and Bacon, 1982), 50.

8. Mary Maud Reed, "An Investigation of the Practice for the Admission of Children and the Promotion of Children from First Grade." (PhD. diss., Teachers College, Columbia University, 1927.

9. Mabel Morphet and Carleton Washburne, "When Should Children Begin to Read?" *Elementary School Journal* 31 (1931): 495–503.

10. Nila Banton Smith, *American Reading Instruction* (Newark, DE: International Reading Association, 1986), 162.

11. Walter Barbe, *Education of the Gifted* (New York: Appleton-Century-Crofts, 1965), 65.

12. Benjamin Bloom, *Stability and Change in Human Characteristics* (New York: Wiley, 1964), 68.

13. Jeanne Chall, *Reading 1967–1977: A Decade of Change and Promise*, The Phi Delta Kappa Educational Foundation, Bloomington, IN, 1977, p. 14.

14. David B. Yaden Jr., Deborah W. Rowe, and Laurie MacGillivray, "Emergent Literacy: A Matter (Polyphony) of Perspectives," in *Handbook of Reading Research*, ed. Michael L. Kamil, Peter Mosenthal, David Pearson, and Rebecca Barr, 3:425–454, 445 (Mahwah, NJ: Erlbaum, 2000).

15. Frank Smith, "Learning to Read by Reading," *Language Arts* 53 (1976): 297–299, 322.

16. William H. Teale and Elizabeth Sulzby, "Emergent Literacy as a Perspective for Examining How Young Children Become Writers and Readers," in *Emergent Literacy*, ed. William Teale and Elizabeth Sulzby, vii–xxv, xx (Norwood, NJ: Ablex, 1986).

17. Lesley M. Morrow, *Literacy Development in the Early Years* (Boston: Allyn and Bacon, 2001), 133–134.

18. See, for example, Dolores Durkin, *Children Who Read Early* (New York: Teachers College Press, 1966).

19. See, for example, Chari Briggs and David Elkind, "Characteristics of Early Readers," *Perceptual and Motor Skills* 44, no. 3 (1977): 1231–1237.

20. Yaden, Rowe, and MacGillvrary, "Emergent Literacy," 437.

21. Ada Anbar, "Natural Reading Acquisition of Preschool Children," *Dissertation Abstracts International, 45*(06), 1700A, 1984, and "Reading Acquisition of Preschool Children without Systematic Instruction," *Early Childhood Research Quarterly* 1 (1986): 69–83; David K. Dickinson and Patton O. Tabors, *Beginning Literacy with Language* (Baltimore: Brookes, 2001); Hope J. Leichter, "Families as Environments for Literacy," in *Awakening to Literacy*, ed. Hillel Goelman, Antoinette Oberg, and Frank Smith, 38–50 (Portsmouth, NH: Heinemann, 1984); Lesley M. Morrow, "Home and School Correlates of Early Interest in Literature," *Journal of Educational Research* 76 (1983): 221–230; Susan B. Neuman, "Guiding Your Children's Participation in Early Literacy Development: A Family Program for Adolescent Mothers," *Early Childhood Development and Care* (1997): 119–129; and William H. Teale, "Reading to Young Children: Its Significance for Literacy Development," in *Awakening to Literacy*, ed. H. Goelman, A. Oberg, and F. Smith, 110–121 (Portsmouth, NH: Heinemann, 1984).

22. Anbar, "Natural Reading," and "Reading Acquisition"; Don Holdaway, "The Structure of Natural Learning as a Basis for Literacy Instruction," in *The Pursuit of Literacy: Early Reading and Writing*, ed. M. Sampson, 56–72 (Dubuque, IA: Kendall/Hunt, 1986); Jana Mason, "When Do Children Begin to Read? An Exploration of Four-Year-Old Children's Letter and Word Reading Competencies," *Reading Research Quarterly* 15 (1980): 203–227; Yetta Goodman, "The Development of Initial Literacy," in *Awakening to Literacy*, ed. H. Goelman, A. Oberg and F. Smith, 102–109 (Exeter, NH: Heinemann, 1984); and Christine E. McCormick and Jana Mason, "What Happens to Kindergarten Children's Knowledge About Reading after Summer Vacation?" *Reading Teacher* 35 (1981): 64–172.

23. Anbar, "Natural Reading."

24. Anbar, "Reading Acquisition," and see chapter 9 of this volume; Kenneth S. Goodman and Yetta M. Goodman, "Learning to Read Is Natural," in *Theory and Practice of Early Reading*, ed. L. B. Resnick and P. A. Weaver, 137–154 (Hillsdale, NJ: Erlbaum, 1979); Margaret Greer Jewell and Miles V. Zintz, *Learning to Read and Write Naturally*, 2nd ed. (Dubuque, IA: Kendall/Hunt, 1990); Huey, *The Psychology and Pedagogy of Reading*; Rebecca S. New, "Early Literacy and Developmentally Appropriate Practice: Rethinking the Paradigm," in *Handbook of Early Literacy Research*, ed. Susan B. Neuman and David K. Dickinson 245–262, 250 (New York: Guilford, 2003);

Frank Smith, ed., *Psycholinguistics and Reading* (New York: Holt, Rinehart and Winston, 1973); and William H. Teale, "Toward a Theory of How Children Learn to Read and Write Naturally," *Language Arts* 59 (1982): 555–570.

25. Anbar, chapter 9, this volume; Anne Forester, "Learning the Language of Reading—An Exploratory Study," *Alberta Journal of Educational Research* 21 (1975): 56–62; Goodman and Goodman, "Learning to Read Is Natural"; Kenneth S. Goodman, "Oral and Written Language: Functions and Purposes," in *Many Families, Many Literacies,* ed. Denny Taylor, 43–46 (Portsmouth, NH: Heinemann Trade, 1997); Jewell and Zintz, *Learning to Read and Write Naturally*; Robert Lado, "Early Reading as Language Development," *Georgetown University Papers in Language and Linguistics* 13 (1976): 8–15, and Ragnhild Soderbergh, *Reading in Early Childhood* (Washington, DC: Georgetown University Press, 1977).

26. Jewell and Zintz, *Learning to Read and Write Naturally*, xix.

27. Lesley M. Morrow, *Literacy Development in the Early Years,* 4th ed. (Boston: Allyn and Bacon, 2001), 61.

28. Gerald Coles, *Reading the Naked Truth* (Portsmouth, NH: Heinemann, 2003).

CHAPTER 9: NATURAL READING DEVELOPMENT

1. Ada Anbar, "Reading Acquisition of Preschool Children without Systematic Instruction," *Early Childhood Research Quarterly* 1 (1986): 69–83.

2. T. Berry Brazelton and Stanley I. Greenspan, *The Irreducible Needs of Children* (Cambridge, MA: Perseus, 2000); and David K. Dickinson and Patton O. Tabors, *Beginning Literacy with Language* (Baltimore: Brookes, 2001).

3. IRA and NAEYC, "Learning to Read and Write: Developmentally Appropriate Practices for Young Children," in *Young Children* 53, no. 4 (1998): 31.

4. Doris Bergen and Juliet Coscia, *Brain Research and Childhood Education* (Olney, MD: Association for Childhood Education International, 2001), 60.

5. William Teale, "Toward a Theory of how Children Learn to Read and Write 'Naturally': An Update," in *Changing Perspective on Research in Reading/Language Processing and Instruction*, 33rd Yearbook

of the National Reading Conference, ed. Jerome Niles, 317, 321, (Rochester, NY: National Reading Conference, 1984).

    6. Joan Beck, *How to Raise a Brighter Child: The Case for Early Learning* (New York: Trident, 1967); Joseph E. Brzeinski and W. Howard, "Early Reading—How, Not When!" *Reading Teacher* 25 (1971): 239–242; J. A. Holmes, "When Should and Could Johnny Learn to Read?" in *Challenge and Experiment in Reading*, ed. Allen J. Figurel, 237–241 (New York: Scholastic Magazine, 1962); Kenneth Hoskisson, "Should Parents Teach Their Children to Read?" *Elementary English* 51 (1974): 295–299; Lloyd O. Ollila, "Pros and Cons of Teaching Reading to Four and Five Year Olds," in *Some Persistent Questions on Beginning Reading*, ed. R.C. Aukerman 53–61 (Newark, DE: International Reading Association, 1972); W. D. Sheldon, "Should the Very Young Be Taught to Read?" *NEA Journal* 52 (1963): 20–24; Wood Smethurst, *Teaching Young Children to Read at Home* (New York: McGraw-Hill, 1975); and George L. Stevens and W. E. Amos, *The Case for Early Reading* (St. Louis: Green, 1968).

    7. Dolores Durkin, *Getting Reading Started* (Boston: Allyn and Bacon, 1982); Yetta Goodman, "Children Coming to Know Literacy," in *Emergent Literacy*, ed. William Teale and Elizabeth Sulzby, 1–14 (Norwood, NJ: Ablex, 1986), and "The Development of Initial Literacy," in *Awakening to Literacy*, ed. H. Goelman, A. Oberg and F. Smith, 102–109 (Portsmouth, NH: Heinemann, 1984); Lesley M. Morrow, *Literacy Development in the Early Years: Helping Children Read and Write* (Needham Heights, MA: Allyn and Bacon, 1989); Joan Brooks McLane and Gillian D. McNamee, *Early Literacy* (Cambridge, MA: Harvard University Press, 1990); Judith A. Schickedanz, "Designing the Early Childhood Classroom Environment to Facilitate Literacy Development," in *Language and Literacy in Early Childhood Education: Yearbook in Early Childhood Education*, vol. 4, ed. Bernard Spodek and Olivia N. Saracho, 141–155 (New York: Teachers College Press, 1993); Dorothy S. Strickland and Lesley Mandel Morrow, eds., *Emerging Literacy: Young Children Learn to Read and Write* (Newark, DE: International Reading Association, 1989); Denny Taylor and Catherine Dorsey-Gaines, *Growing Up Literate* (Portsmouth, NH: Heinemann, 1988); William Teale and Elizabeth Sulzby, eds., *Emergent Literacy* (Norwood, NJ: Ablex, 1986); and William Teale, "Emergent Literacy: Reading and Writing Development in Early Childhood," in *36th Yearbook of the National Reading Conference* (Rochester, NY: National Reading Conference, 1987), 45–74.

8. Elsa Auerbach, "Reading between the Lines," in *Many Families, Many Literacies*, ed. Denny Taylor, 71–81, 75 (Portsmouth, NH: Heinemann, 1997).

9. Jeanne R. Paratore, Gigliana Melzi, and Barbara Krol-Sinclair, "Learning about the Literate Lives of Latino Families," in *Literacy and Young Children*, ed. Diane M. Barone and Lesley Mandel Morrow, 101–118, 117 (New York: Guilford, 2003).

10. Carl Bereiter, *Must We Educate?* (Englewood Cliffs, NJ: Prentice-Hall, 1973), 57.

11. Denny Taylor, ed. *Many Families, Many Literacies* (Portsmouth, NH: Heinemann Trade, 1997).

12. Ibid., back cover.

13. Susan B. Neuman, "How Can We Enable All Children to Achieve," in *Children Achieving*, ed. Susan B. Neuman and Kathleen A. Roskos, 5–19, 13 (Newark, DE: International Reading Association, 1998).

14. Peter Hannon, *Literacy, Home, and School* (London: Falmer Press, 1995); Paratore, Melzi, and Krol-Sinclair, "Learning about the Literate Lives of Latino Families"; Taylor, ed., *Many Families, Many Literacies*; and G. Valdes, *Con respeto: Bridging the Differences between Culturally Diverse Families and Schools* (New York: Teachers College Press, 1996).

15. Diane Barone, "How Do We Teach Literacy to Children Who Are Learning English as a Second Language?" in *Children Achieving*, ed. Susan B. Neuman and Kathleen A. Roskos, 56–76, 57 (Newark, DE: International Reading Association, 1998).

16. Bergen and Coscia, *Brain Research and Childhood Education*, 23.

17. Ibid., 57.

18. Barone, "How Do We Teach Literacy," 57.

19. Ibid.

20. Marilyn Jager Adams, *Beginning to Read: Thinking and Learning about Print* (Cambridge, MA: MIT Press,1990); B. Blachman, "Phonological Awareness," in *Handbook of Reading Research*, vol. 3, ed. Michael Kamil, Peter Mosenthal, David Pearson, and Rebecca Barr, 483–502 (Mahwah, NJ: Erlbaum, 2000); Usha Goswami, "Early Phonological Development and the Acquisition of Literacy," in *Handbook of Early Literacy Research*, ed. Susan B. Neweman and David K. Dickinson 111–125 (New York: Guilford, 2003); and Darrell Morris and Janet Bloodgood, "Developmental Steps in Learning to Read: A Longitudinal

Study in Kindergarten and First Grade," *Reading Research Quarterly* 38, no. 3 (2003): 302–328.

21. Jeanne Chall, *Learning to Read: The Great Debate* (New York: McGraw-Hill, 1967).

22. Lesley M. Morrow, *Literacy Development in the Early Years*, 4th ed. (Boston: Allyn and Bacon, 2001), 42.

23. Ibid., 143.

CHAPTER 10: TO TAKE THE NATURAL COURSE OR NOT

1. Ada Anbar, "Preschool Education in Other Countries," in *How to Choose a Nursery School* (Palo Alto, CA: Pacific Books, 1999), 117–157, 127; Takahiko Sakamoto, "Preschool Reading in Japan," *Reading Teacher* 29 (1975): 240–244; and Takahiko Sakamoto and K. Makita, *Japan in Comparative Reading*, ed. J. Downing, 440–465 (New York: Macmillan, 1973).

2. Shoshana Matzner-Bekerman, *The Jewish Child* (New York: KTAV, 1984), 233.

3. Anbar, "Preschool Education in Other Countries," 134; and Joseph J. Tobin, David Y. H. Wu, and Dana H. Davidson, *Preschool in Three Cultures* (New Haven, CT: Yale University Press, 1989), 123.

4. Ada Anbar, "Reading Acquisition of Preschool Children without Systematic Instruction," *Early Childhood Research Quarterly* 1 (1986): 69–83; J. E. Brzienski and W. Howard, "Early Reading—How, Not When," *Reading Teacher* 25 (1971): 239–242; Margaret Clark, *Young Fluent Readers* (London: Heinemann Educational Books, 1976); Dolores Durkin, *Children Who Read Early* (New York: Teachers College Press, 1966), and "A Six Year Study of Children Who Learned to Read in School at the Age of Four," *Reading Research Quarterly* 10, no. 1 (1974–1975): 9–61, 9; Bonnie Lass, "Portrait of My Son as an Early Reader," *Reading Teacher* (October 1982): 20–28; and Wood Smethurst, *Teaching Young Children to Read at Home* (New York: McGraw-Hill, 1975).

5. Ada Anbar, "Children's Play," in *How to Choose a Nursery School*, 2nd ed. (Palo Alto, CA: Pacific Books, 1999), 76–87.

6. David Elkind, "Thanks for the Memory: The Lasting Value of True Play," *Young Children* 58, no. 3, (2003): 46–50.

7. David Dickinson, "Large-Group and Free-Play Times: Conversational Settings Supporting Language and Literacy Develop-

ment," in *Beginning Literacy with Language,* ed. David K. Dickinson and Patton O. Tabors, 223–255 (Baltimore: Brookes, 2001); Nigel Hall, "Literacy, Play, and Authentic Experience," in *Play and Literacy in Early Childhood,* ed. Kathleen A. Roskos and James F. Christie, 189–204 (Mahwah, NJ: Erlbaum, 2000); Elizabeth Jones, "Playing to Get Smart," *Young Children* 58, no. 3 (2003) 32–36; Lea M. McGee, "Book Acting: Storytelling and Drama in the Early Childhood Classroom," in *Literacy and Young Children*, ed. Diane M. Barone and Lesley Mandel Morrow, 157–170 (New York: Guilford, 2003); Gretchen Owocki, *Literacy through Play* (Portsmouth, NH: Heinemann, 1999); Kathleen A. Roskos and James F. Christie, *Play and Literacy in Early Childhood* (Mahwah, NJ: Erlbaum, 2000); and Marian Whitehead, "Play and Language," in *Supporting Language and Literacy Development in the Early Years* (Philadelphia: Open University Press, 1999): 16–26.

8. Doris Bergen., ed. *Play as a Medium for Learning and Development: A Handbook of Theory and Practice* (Portsmouth, NH: Heinemann, 1987); D. P. Fromberg, *Play and Meaning in Early Childhood Education* (Boston: Allyn and Bacon, 2001); and J. Frost, S. Wortham, and S. Reifel, *Play and Child Development* (Upper Saddle River, NJ: Merrill/Prentice-Hall, 2001).

9. Ada Anbar, "Four Approaches to Preschool Education," in *How to Choose a Nursery School* (Palo Alto, CA: Pacific Books, 1999), 26–55; and Catherine Lewis, *Educating Hearts and Minds* (New York: Cambridge University Press, 1995).

10. Kathleen A. Roskos and James F. Christie, eds. *Play and Literacy in Early Childhood* (Mahwah, NJ: Erlbaum, 2000), 240.

11. David Elkind, *The Hurried Child* (Reading, MA: Addison-Wesley, 1981).

12. Clark, *Young Fluent Readers*; and Durkin, "A Six Year Study."

13. Julee J. Newberger, "New Brain Development Research—A Wonderful Window of Opportunity to Build Public Support for Early Childhood Education," *Young Children* 52, no. 4 (1997): 4–9, 5.

14. Doris Bergen and Juliet Coscia, *Brain Research and Childhood Education* (Olney, MD: Association for Childhood Education International, 2001), 23.

15. Sarah Friedman and Rodney Cocking, "Instructional Influences on Cognition and on the Brain," in *The Brain, Cognition, and Education,* ed. Sarah Friedman, Kenneth A. Klivington, and Rita W. Peterson, 319–343, 319 (Orlando, FL: Academic, 1986).

16. Howard Gardner, "Notes on Cognitive Development: Recent Trends, New Directions," in *The Brain, Cognition, and Education,* ed. Sarah Friedman, Kenneth A. Klivington, and Rita W. Peterson, 259–285, 270 (Orlando, FL: Academic, 1986).

17. Benjamin Bloom, *Stability and Change in Human Characteristics* (New York: Wiley, 1964), 68.

18. Bergen and Coscia, *Brain Research and Childhood Education,* 60.

19. Ibid., 66.

20. John Eccles and Daniel Robinson, *The Wonder of Being Human* (Boston: New Science Library, 1984), 114.

21. Robert Lado, "Early Reading as Language Development," *Georgetown University Papers on Language and Linguistics* 13 (1976): 8–15; Ragnhild Soderbergh, "Learning to Read: Breaking the Code or Acquiring Functional Literacy," *Georgetown University Papers on Languages and Linguistics* 13 (1976): 16–34; and George L. Stevens and W. E. Amos, *The Case of Early Reading* (St. Louis: Green, 1968).

22. Lise Eliot, *What's Going On in There?* (New York: Bantam Books, 2000), 364.

23. Bergen and Coscia, *Brain Research and Childhood Education,* 25.

24. Anbar, "Four Approaches to Preschool Education."

25. Stephen R. Burgess, Steven A. Hecht, Christopher J. Lonigan, "Relations of the Home Literacy Environment (HLE) to the Development of Reading-Related Abilities: A One-Year Longitudinal Study," *Reading Research Quarterly* 37, no. 4 (2002): 408–426.

26. William H. Teale, "Questions about Early Literacy Learning and Teaching That Need Asking—and Some That Don't," in *Literacy and Young Children,* ed. Diane M. Barone and Lesley Mandel Morrow, 23–44, 23 (New York: Guilford, 2003).

27. Ursula Kirk, *Neuorpsychology of Language, Reading, and Spelling* (New York: Elsevire Science and Technology Books, 1983), 262.

28. Matthew Melmed, "Parents Speak: Zero to Three's Findings from Research on Parents' Views of Early Childhood Development," *Young Children* 52, no. 5 (1997): 46–49, 48.

29. Michelle V. Porche, "Parent Involvement as a Link between Home and School," in *Beginning Literacy with Language,* ed. David K. Dickinson and Patton O. Tabors, 291–312, 312 (Baltimore: Brookes, 2001).

CHAPTER 11: HOW, WHEN, AND WHERE

1. Peggy Kay, *Games for Reading* (New York: Pantheon Books, 1984); Jill Frankel Hauser, *Growing up Reading—Learning to Read through Creative Play* (Charlotte, VT: Williamson, 1993); Gretchen Owocki, *Literacy through Play* (Portsmouth, NH: Heinemann, 1999); Kathleen A. Roskos and James F. Christie, eds., *Play and Literacy in Early Childhood* (Mahwah, NJ: Erlbaum, 2000); and Judith A. Schickedanz, "Engaging Preschoolers in Code Learning: Some Thoughts about Preschool Teachers' Concerns," in *Literacy and Young Children*, ed. Diane M. Barone and Lesley Mandel Morrow, 121–139 (New York: Guilford, 2003).

2. Gretchen Owocki and Yetta Goodman, *Kidwatching* (Portsmouth, NH: Heinemann, 2002).

3. Ken Goodman, "Oral and Written Language: Functions and Purposes," in *Many Families, Many Literacies*, ed. Denny Taylor, 43–46 (Portsmouth, NH: Heinemann, 1997).

Selected Bibliography

Adams, Marilyn Jager. *Beginning to Read.* Cambridge, MA: MIT Press, 1990.

Anbar, Ada. *How to Choose a Nursery School.* 2nd ed. Palo Alto, CA: Pacific Books, 1999.

———. "Natural Reading Acquisition of Preschool Children." *Dissertation Abstracts International,* 45 (06), 1700A, 1984.

———. "Reading Acquisition of Preschool Children without Systematic Instruction." *Early Childhood Research Quarterly* 1 (1986): 69–83.

Bailey, Donald B., John T. Bruer, Frank J. Symons, and Jeff W. Lichtman, eds. *Critical Thinking about Critical Periods.* Baltimore: Brookes, 2001.

Barone, Diane. "How Do We Teach Literacy to Children Who Are Learning English as a Second Language?" In *Children Achieving,* ed. Susan B. Neuman and Kathleen A. Roskos, 56–76. Newark, DE: International Reading Association, 1998.

Barone, Diane M., and Lesley Mandel Morrow, eds. *Literacy and Young Children.* New York: Guilford, 2003.

Bereiter, Carl. *Must We Educate?* Englewood Cliffs, NJ: Prentice-Hall, 1973.

Bergen, Doris, and Juliet Coscia. *Brain Research and Childhood Education.* Olney, MD: Association for Childhood Education International, 2001.

Bissex, Glenda L. *Gnys at Wrk.* Cambridge, MA: Harvard University Press, 1980.

Brzienski, Joseph E., and W. Howard. "Early Reading—How, Not When." *Reading Teacher* 25 (1971): 239–242.

Cairney, Trevor H. "Literacy within Family Life." In *Handbook of Early Childhood Literacy*, ed. Nigel Hall, Joanne Larson, and Jackie Marsh, 85–98. London: Sage, 2003.

Cambourne, Brian. "Taking a Naturalistic Viewpoint in Early Childhood Literacy Research." In *Handbook of Early Childhood Literacy*, ed. Nigel Hall, Joanne Larson, and Jackie Marsh, 411–423. London: Sage, 2003.

Campbell, Robin, ed. *Facilitating Preschool Literacy.* Newark, DE: International Reading Association, 1998.

Chall, Jeanne S., Vicki A. Jacobs, and Luke E. Baldwin. *The Reading Crisis.* Cambridge, MA: Harvard University Press, 1990.

Christie, James F., ed. *Play and Early Literacy Development.* Albany, NY: State University of New York Press, 1991.

Clark, Margaret. *Young Fluent Readers.* London: Heinemann Educational Books, 1976.

Clay, Marie M. *Becoming Literate: The Construction of Inner Controls.* Portsmouth, NH: Heinemann, 1991.

———. *Reading: The Patterning of Complex Behavior.* Auckland, New Zealand: Heinemann Educational Books, 1972.

———. *What Did I Write?* Auckland, New Zealand: Heinemann Educational Books, 1975.

Coles, Gerald. *Reading the Naked Truth.* Portsmouth, NH: Heinemann, 2003.

Dickinson, David K., and Miriam W. Smith. "Supporting Language and Literacy Development in the Preschool Classroom." In *Beginning Literacy with Language*, ed. David Dickinson and Patton O. Tabors, 139–147. Baltimore: Brookes, 2001.

Dickinson, David K., and Patton O. Tabors. *Beginning Literacy with Language.* Baltimore: Brookes, 2001.

Dunn, Loraine, Sara Ann Beach, and Susan Kontos. "Supporting Literacy in Early Childhood Programs: A Challenge for the Future." In *Play and Literacy in Early Childhood*, ed. Kathleen A. Roskos and James F. Christie, 91–105. Mahwah, NJ: Erlbaum, 2000.

Durkin, Dolores. *Children Who Read Early.* New York: Teachers College Press, 1966.

———. *Getting Reading Started.* Boston: Allyn and Bacon, 1982.

Eccles, John C. *Evolution of the Brain: Creation of the Self.* London: Routledge, 1991.

Eccles, John, and Daniel Robinson. *The Wonder of Being Human.* Boston: New Science Library, 1984.

Eliot, Lise. *What's Going On in There?* New York: Bantam Books, 2000.

Figurel, Allen J., ed. *Challenge and Experiment in Reading.* New York: Scholastic Magazine, 1962.

Fillmer, Thompson H., and Bill Cole Cliett. *Nurturing Your Child's Natural Literacy.* Gainesville, FL: Maupin House, 1992.

Flippo, Rona F. *What Do the Experts Say?* Portsmouth, NH: Heinemann, 1999.

Flurkey, Alan D., and Jingguo Xu, eds. *On the Revolution of Reading.* Portsmouth, NH: Heinemann, 2003.

Forester, Anne. "What Teachers Can Learn from Natural Readers." *Reading Teacher* 31 (1977): 160–166.

Friedman, Sarah L., Kenneth A. Klivington, and Rita W. Peterson, eds. *The Brain, Cognition, and Education.* Orlando, FL: Academic, 1986.

Fromkin, Victoria, and Robert Rodman. *An Introduction to Language,* 5th ed. Orlando, FL: Harcourt Brace Jovanovich, 1993.

Gardner, Howard. "Notes on Cognitive Development: Recent Trends, New Directions." In *The Brain, Cognition, and Education,* ed. Sarah L. Friedman, Kenneth A. Klivington, and Rita W. Peterson, 259–285. Orlando, FL: Academic, 1986.

Goodman, Kenneth S., and Yeta Goodman. "Learning to Read is Natural." In *Theory and Practice of Early Reading,* ed. Lauren B. Resnick and Phyllis A. Weaver, 137–154. Hillsdale, NJ: Erlbaum, 1979.

Goodman, Yeta. "Children Coming to Know Literacy." In *Emergent Literacy,* ed. William H. Teale and Elizabeth Sulzby, 1–14. Norwood, NJ: Ablex, 1986.

———. "The Development of Initial Literacy." In *Awakening to Literacy,* ed. Hillel Goelman, Antoinette Oberg, and Frank Smith, 102–109. Portsmouth, NH: Heinemann, 1984.

———. "The Roots of Literacy." In *Claremont Reading Conference 44th Yearbook,* ed. Malcolm P. Douglass, 1–32. Claremont, CA: Claremont Reading Conference, 1980.

Gordon, Edward E., and Elaine H. Gordon. *Literacy in America.* Westport, CT: Praeger, 2003.

Hall, Nigel. "Literacy, Play, and Authentic Experience." In *Play and Literacy in Early Childhood*, ed. Kathleen A. Roskos and James F. Christie, 189–204. Mahwah, NJ: Erlbaum, 2000.

Hall, Nigel, Joanne Larson, and Jackie Marsh, eds. *Handbook of Early Childhood Literacy*. London: Sage, 2003.

Hannon, Peter. "Family Literacy Programs." In *Handbook of Early Childhood Literacy*, ed. Nigel Hall, Joanne Larson, and Jackie Marsh, 99–111. London: Sage, 2003.

———. *Literacy, Home and School*. London: Falmer, 1995.

———. *Reflecting on Literacy in Education*. London: Routledge Falmer, 2000.

Harris, William V. *Ancient Literacy*. Cambridge, Massachusetts: Harvard University Press, 1989.

Hauser, Jill Frankel. *Growing Up Reading—Learning to Read through Creative Play*. Charlotte, VT: Willamson, 1993.

Holdaway, Don. *The Foundations of Literacy*. Sydney, Australia: Ashton Scholastic, 1979.

Huey, Edmund B. *The Psychology and Pedagogy of Reading*. New York: Macmillan, 1908. Reprinted Cambridge, MA: MIT Press, 1968. Page references are to the 1968 edition.

Jackendoff, Ray. *Patterns in the Mind*. New York: Basic Books, 1994.

Jackson, Donald. *The Story of Writing*. New York: Taplinger, 1981.

Jewell, Margaret Greer, and Miles V. Zintz. *Learning to Read and Write Naturally*, 2nd ed. Dubuque, IA: Kendall/Hunt, 1990.

Kamil, Michael, Peter Mosenthal, David Pearson, and Rebecca Barr, eds. *Handbook of Reading Research*, vol. 3. Mahwah, NJ: Erlbaum, 2000.

Klein, Tovah P. "Play: Children's Context for Development." *Young Children* 58, no. 3 (2003):38–45.

Labbo, Linda D., and David Reinking. "Computers and Early Literacy Education." In *Handbook of Early Childhood Literacy*, ed. Nigel Hall, Joanne Larson, and Jackie Marsh, 338–354. London: Sage, 2003.

Lado, Robert. "Early Reading as Language Development." *Georgetown University Papers in Language and Linguistics* 13 (1976): 8–15.

Makin, Laurie. "Creating Positive Literacy Learning Environments in Early Childhood." In *Handbook of Early Childhood Literacy* ed. Nigel Hall, Joanne Larson, and Jackie Marsh, 327–337. London: Sage, 2003.

Manguel, Alberto. *A History of Reading*. New York: Viking, 1996.

Martens, Prisca. "Growing as a Reader and Writer: Sarah's Inquiry into Literacy." In *Facilitating Preschool Literacy*. Newark, DE: International Reading Association, 1998, 51–68.

Mason, Jana. "When Do Children Begin to Read? An Exploration of Four-Year-Old Children's Letter and Word Reading Competencies." *Reading Research Quarterly* 15 (1980): 203–227.

McGee, Lea M. "Book Acting: Storytelling and Drama in the Early Childhood Classroom." In *Literacy and Young Children*, ed. Diane M. Barone and Lesley Mandel Morrow, 157–170. New York: Guilford, 2003.

McLane, Joan Brooks, and Gillian D. McNamee. *Early Literacy*. Cambridge, MA: Harvard University Press, 1990.

McNaughton, Stuart. *Patterns of Emergent Literacy*. Melbourne, Australia: Oxford University Press, 1995.

McQuillan, Jeff. *The Literacy Crisis*. Portsmouth, NH: Heinemann, 1998.

Minns, Hilary. *Read It to Me Now!* Buckingham, UK: Open University Press, 1997.

Morrow, Lesley M. *Family Literacy Connections at School and Home*. Newark, DE: International Reading Association. 1995.

———. *Literacy Development in the Early Years*. 4th ed. Boston: Allyn and Bacon, 2001.

Neuman, Susan B. "Guiding Your Children's Participation in Early Literacy Development: A Family Program for Adolescent Mothers." *Early Childhood Development and Care* (1997): 119–129.

———. "How Can We Enable All Children to Achieve." In *Children Achieving*, ed. Susan B. Neuman and Kathleen A. Roskos, 5–19. Newark, DE: International Reading Association, 1998.

———. "Social Contexts for Literacy Development: A Family Literacy Program." In *Play and Literacy in Early Childhood*, ed. Kathleen A. Roskos and James F. Christie, 153–168. Mahwah, NJ: Erlbaum, 2000.

Neuman, Susan B., and David K. Dickinson, eds. *Handbook of Early Literacy Research*. New York: Guilford, 2003.

Neuman, Susan B., and Kathleen A. Roskos, eds. *Children Achieving*. Newark, DE: International Reading Association, 1998.

Neville, Helen J., and John T. Bruer. "Language Processing: How Experience Affects Brain Organization." In *Critical Thinking about Critical Periods*, ed. Donald B. Bailey, John T. Bruer, Frank J. Symons, and Jeff W. Lichtman. 151–172. Baltimore: Brookes, 2001.

Newberger, Julee J. "New Brain Development Research—A Wonderful Window of Opportunity to Build Public Support for Early Childhood Education." *Young Children* 52, no. 4 (1997): 4–9.

Nicholson, Tom. "Literacy in the Family and Society." In *Learning to Read*, ed. G. Brian Thompson and Tom Nicholson, 1–22. New York: Teachers College Press, 1999.

Osherson, Daniel N., and Howard Lasnik, eds. *Language*. Vol 1. Cambridge, MA: MIT Press, 1990.

Owocki, Gretchen. "Developing the Literate Play Environment." In *Literacy through Play*. Portsmouth, NH: Heinemann, 1999, 102–121.

———. *Literacy through Play*. Portsmouth, NH: Heinemann, 1999.

Owocki, Gretchen, and Yetta Goodman. *Kidwatching*. Portsmouth, NH: Heinemann, 2002.

Paratore, Jeanne R., Gigliana Melzi, and Barbara Krol-Sinclair. "Learning about the Literate Lives of Latino Families." In *Literacy and Young Children*, ed. Diane M. Barone and Lesley Mandel Morrow, 101–118. New York: Guilford, 2003.

Pellegrini, A. D., and Lee Galda. "Commentary—Cognitive Development, Play, and Literacy: Issues of Defenition and Developmental Function." In *Play and Literacy in Early Childhood*, ed. Kathleen A. Roskos and James F. Christie, 63–74. Mahwah, NJ: Erlbaum, 2000.

Pflaum, Susanna W. *The Development of Language and Literacy in Young Children*. Columbus, OH: Merrill, 1986.

Reichmann, Felix. *The Sources of Western Literacy*. Westport, CT: Greenwood, 1980.

Resnick, Lauren, and Phyllis Weaver, eds. *Theory and Practice of Early Reading*. Vol. 1. Hillsdale, NJ: Erlbaum, 1979.

Robinson, Andrew. *The Story of Writing*. London: Thames and Hudson, 1995.

Roskos, Kathleen A. "Through the Bioecological Lens: Some Observations of Literacy In Play as a Proximal Process." In *Play and Literacy in Early Childhood*, ed. Kathleen A. Roskos and James F. Christie, 125–137. Mahwah, NJ: Erlbaum, 2000.

Roskos, Kathleen A., and James F. Christie, eds. *Play and Literacy in Early Childhood*. Mahwah, NJ: Erlbaum, 2000.

Ruddell, Robert B., Martha Rapp Ruddell, and Harry Singer, eds. *Theoretical Models and Processes of Reading*. 4th ed. Newark, DE: International Reading Association, 1994.

Sampson, Geoffrey. *Writing Systems*. Stanford, CA: Stanford University Press, 1985.

Sampson, M., ed. *The Pursuit of Literacy: Early Reading and Writing*. Dubuque, IA: Kendall/Hunt, 1986.

Schickedanz, Judith A. *Adam's Righting Revolutions*. Portsmouth, NH: Heinemann, 1990.

———. "Engaging Preschoolers in Code Learning: Some Thoughts about Preschool Teachers' Concerns." In *Literacy and Young Children*, ed. Diane M. Barone and Lesley Mandel Morrow, 121–139. New York: Guilford, 2003.

———. *Much More Than the ABCs*. Washington, DC: National Association for the Education of Young Children, 1999.

Schmandt-Besserat, Denise. *How Writing Came About*. Austin: University of Texas Press, 1992.

Schwartz, Judith. *Encouraging Early Literacy*. Portsmouth, NH: Heinemann, 1988.

Smethurst, Wood. *Teaching Young Children to Read at Home*. New York: McGraw-Hill, 1975.

Smith, Frank, ed. *Psycholinguistics and Reading*. New York: Holt, Rinehart, and Winston, 1973.

Smith, Nila Banton. *American Reading Instruction*. Newark, DE: International Reading Association, 1986.

Stevens, George L., and W. E. Amos. *The Case of Early Reading*. St. Louis: Green, 1968.

Street, Brian V., ed. *Literacy and Development*. London: Routledge, 2001.

Strickland, Dorothy S., and Lesley Mandel Morrow, eds. *Emerging Literacy: Young Children Learn to Read and Write*. Newark, DE: International Reading Association, 1989.

Tabors, Patton O., and Catherine E. Snow. "Young Bilingual Children and Early Literacy Development." In *Handbook of Early Literacy Research*, ed. Susan B. Neuman and David K. Dickinson, 159–178. New York: Guilford, 2003.

Taylor, Denny. *Family Literacy*. Exeter, NH: Heinemann, 1983.

———, ed. *Many Families, Many Literacies*. Portsmouth, NH: Heinemann, 1997.

Taylor, Denny, and Catherine Dorsey-Gaines. *Growing Up Literate*. Portsmouth, NH: Heinemann, 1988.

Teale, William. "Emergent Literacy: Reading and Writing Development in Early Childhood." In *36th Yearbook of the National Reading*

Conference. Rochester, NY: National Reading Conference, 1987. 45–74.

———. "Questions about Early Literacy Learning and Teaching That Need Asking—and Some That Don't." In *Literacy and Young Children*, ed. Diane M. Barone and Lesley M. Morrow, 23–44. New York: Guilford, 2003.

———. "Toward a Theory of How Children Learn to Read and Write Naturally." *Language Arts* 59 (1982): 555–570.

———. "Toward a Theory of How Children Learn to Read and Write 'Naturally': An Update." In *Changing Perspective on Research in Reading/Language Processing and Instruction*, 33rd Yearbook of the National Reading Conference. Edited by J. Niles (1984): pp. 317–322.

Teale, William H., and Elizabeth Sulzby, eds. *Emergent Literacy*. Norwood, NJ: Ablex, 1986.

Torrey, Jane. "Reading That Comes Naturally: The Early Reader." In *Reading Research*, Vol. 1, ed. T. Gary Walter and G. E. Mackinnon, 115–144. New York: Academic, 1979.

Index

parent–teacher collaboration, 171, 175, 186–187

phonemic awareness and phonics, 98; and natural reading development, 114, 155–157

phonographic script, 7

physical development, 163

Piaget, Jean, 161

pictograms, 7

Plato, 10, 161

play: definition of, 162; and early reading development, 28, 83–84, 94, 97, 122, 129, 130–133, 135, 145, 161, 171; free play, 162; games for reading development, 156, 184 (*see also* reading games); importance of, 161–163

Porche, Michelle, 175

preschool and early reading development, 26, 65, 109, 185; academic-oriented preschool, 161, 169; objective, 169–171; traditional American nursery school, 162, 170, 185

preschool teachers and early reading development, 29, 170, 171; recommendations, 186; role of, 175, 185–186

public library, use of, and early reading development, 46, 61, 64, 98–99, 129–130; in ancient times, 8

reading, history of: beginnings, 5; Bible, effect of, 11; bones with tally marks, 4; cave paintings, 4; clay tokens, 5; cuneiform script, 7–8; democracy and reading, 10; future of, 14–15; Greek alphabet, 10; hieroglyphs, 7–8; modern times, 14; Phoenician alpha-

bet, 9; printing press, effect of, 12–13; Renaissance, 12; Roman Church and reading, 11

reading acquisition, when does it start: emergent literacy perspective, 23–24; before the era of compulsory education, 17–19; natural reading development, 26–29; reading readiness perspective, 20–22. *See also* early readers

reading activities, informal beginning of: alphabet blocks, 44, 72, 119; bedtime story, 134, 183; cards for reading, 60–61; dramatic play, 24, 64; flash cards, of letters, of words, 44, 48, 94; flipping through books, 112, 119, 127; grocery lists, 99; letters to grandma, 99; magnetic letters on the refrigerator, 42, 63; making words, 50, 66, 79, 115, 120, 133; messages to a preschool child, 78, 80; names of the letters, learning of, 64, 66, 76, 115; nursery rhymes, 63, 67, 130; pointing at the print while reading to the child, 66, 81, 121; pointing out direction words, 60, 78; pointing out storefront names, 60; pointing out traffic signs, 44; pointing out words in advertisements; puzzles, 144; shapes, learning of, 66; sounds of the letters, learning of, 45, 60, 66, 99; storybook readings, 24, 44, 62, 81, 97, 182; subscriptions to a book club, or children's magazine, 61, 118; this is a capital A, and this is a

ABOUT THE AUTHOR

ADA ANBAR holds a Ph.D. in Early Childhood Education from the State University of New York, Buffalo, and, after a 40-year teaching career, is now a full-time writer.